Institutional Trauma

Institutional
Trauma

Major Change in Museums and Its Effect on Staff

Elaine Heumann Gurian, Editor

American Association of Museums
Washington, D.C.
1995

INSTITUTIONAL TRAUMA
Major Change in Museums and Its Effect on Staff

Institutional trauma : major change in museums and its effect on staff
      / Elaine Heumann Gurian, editor.
              p.   cm.
       Includes bibliographical references and index.
       ISBN 0-931201-19-5 (hard). — ISBN 0-931201-20-9 (paper)
       1. Museums—United States—Management—Social aspects.
    2. Museums—Philosophy. 3. Social change—United States—History.
    I. Gurian, Elaine Heumann, 1937-   . II. American Association of Museums.
    AM11.I59 1995
      069'.0973—dc20   95-16234
                                                          CIP

Contents

Institutional Trauma

Authors

Joseph G. Ansel, Jr. worked for nearly 20 years at The Exploratorium. He held three positions: exhibit shop manager/exhibit designer, fund raiser and administrator and marketing executive. He served as a member of the Executive Council, the Exploratorium's managing body, prior to and during the initial stages of the institution's unionization. In August 1992, Ansel left the Exploratorium to establish his own consulting and design practice, Ansel Associates. Among his clients are American science centers, the state of California and the government of Saudi Arabia. He holds a B.S. in management from the University of Santa Clara.

John R. Brumgardt has been director of The Charleston Museum since 1984. He began his career in 1974 with the Riverside (Calif.) Municipal Museum and subsequently served as head of the history division for the Riverside County Parks Department and as director of the Museum of Western Colorado. Brumgardt has served as vice president and acting chairman of the Colorado Humanities Committee, president of the Mountain-Plains Museums Association and the South Carolina Federation of Museums and treasurer of the Southeastern Museums Conference. He holds a Ph.D. in history from the University of California, an honorary doctorate of letters from the College of Charleston and a management development certificate from the University of Colorado. In addition to papers and articles on museum management, his publications include *Civil War Nurse: The Diary and Letters of Hannah Ropes* (University of Tennessee Press, 1981) and numerous articles concerning Civil War and California history.

Rina Bar-Lev Elieli is a psychoanalyst, clinical psychologist and organizational consultant. She is active in several organizations that focus on the role of psychoanalysis in organizational studies. As a consultant, Elieli has worked with a variety of organizations, including those in industry, health, art, education, the military and banking. She has worked internationally and in Israel, where she lives. Elieli is on the faculty of the School of Psychotherapy at the Tel-Aviv University Medical School and teaches at the Israeli Polytechnic Institute.

Laurence J. Gould, principal, Gould Krantz White, Inc., is a training and organizational development specialist. He has worked with both private and public sector clients including General Electric, the Juilliard School of Music, the United States Holocaust Memorial Museum, New York Hospital, ITT Financial Services, Sheraton, the American Psychological Association, the Discovery Networks and the Executive Office of the President. These projects include organization and work redesign, team training and executive team development, and the design and implementation of team-based organizations. He is a professor of psychology at the City University of New York and the director of the Organizational Consultation Service of the Program in Organizational Development Consultation at the William Alanson White Institute.

Elaine Heumann Gurian is an advisor/consultant to museums that are beginning, building or reinventing themselves, including the Museum of New Zealand and the National Arts Council, Mauritius. She has participated in five museum projects, each undergoing various stages of change. At The Children's Museum, Boston, Gurian was director, exhibit center from 1972-85 and associate director from 1985-87. As the deputy assistant secretary for museums at the Smithsonian Institution (1987-1990), she was the lead staff person for the African-American Museum Project and the Experimental Gallery. Gurian was deputy director for public program planning at the National Museum of the American Indian (1990-91) and deputy director, United States Holocaust Memorial Museum (1991-94). She has also served as vice president, treasurer and council member of the American Association of Museums.

Holly Hotchner worked at the New-York Historical Society from 1984 to 1994. She was hired as the Society's chief conservator and in 1988 was named director of the museum. Previously, she was a Sherman Fairchild Conservation Fellow at the Metropolitan Museum of Art, New York. Hotchner trained in the conservation of modern paintings at the Tate Gallery, London, and the Hirshhorn Museum and Sculpture Garden in Washington, D.C. Before becoming a conservator, she worked in exhibitions and registration at the Museum of Modern Art, New York. A native of New York City, Hotchner holds a B.A. in art history and studio art from Trinity College, and received her M.A. in art history and a degree in conservation from the Institute of Fine Arts, New York University.

Suzanne LeBlanc currently serves as executive director of the Lied Discovery Children's Museum in Las Vegas, Nev. She was previously an assistant director at The Brooklyn Children's Museum, and worked for 15 years in a variety of positions at The Children's Museum, Boston. She attended the Museum Management Institute in July 1987 and received an M.A. in counseling psychology from Lesley College and a B.S. in journalism from Boston University. She is currently one of three vice presidents of the Association of Youth Museums and president of the Nevada Museums Association.

Kathleen McLean was appointed director of public programs and the head of the Center for Public Exhibition at The Exploratorium in January 1994. She is principal of Independent Exhibitions, a museum exhibition consulting firm, and has previously held positions as director of exhibits and publications at the Maryland Science Center; director of exhibitions and publications at The Brooklyn Children's Museum; and museum curatorial specialist at The Oakland Museum. She is the author of the book *Planning for People in Museum Exhibitions,* and editor of *Recent and Recommended: A Museum Exhibition Bibliography with Notes from the Field.*

Patrick Norris has been director of the Kalamazoo Public Museum since 1985. Previously, he was director of Chippewa Valley Museum and curator of history at the Fort Worth Museum of Science and History. He received a doctorate in American studies from the University of Minnesota and is an adjunct professor of history at Western Michigan University, where he teaches courses in museum studies. He is the author of *History By Design: A Primer on Interpreting and Exhibiting Community History* (Texas Association of Museums, 1985). He has also taught at the University of Maryland and Texas Christian University.

Judith Hansen O'Toole is currently director/CEO of the Westmoreland Museum of Art in Greenburg, Pa. She received a master's degree in art history from the Pennsylvania State University. O'Toole was director of the Sordoni Art Gallery, Wilkes University in Wilkes-Barre, Pa., from 1982 until 1993. She has lectured and published in the field of American art, including a monograph on Severin Roesen (Bucknell University Press, 1982) and numerous exhibition catalogues, including two on "Ash Can" painter George Luks.

Talbert Spence is vice president of the education division at the National Audubon Society in New York. Over the past 20 years in the New York City area, he has served in positions at the American Museum of Natural History, the New York Academy of

Sciences and Wave Hill Public Garden. Spence received his bachelor's of education from the University of Toledo in Ohio and an M.S. in natural resource management from the University of Michigan. He has been a science teacher in the Toledo Public Schools and has served as an adjunct and visiting professor and lecturer at Barnard College, the City College of New York, the National Faculty Program at Evergreen State College in Olympia, Wash., and the University of Oregon, Eugene.

Rowena Stewart is director of the Motown Historical Museum in Detroit. Previously, she was executive director of the Afro-American Historical and Cultural Museum in Philadelphia (1985-1992) and founder of the Rhode Island Black Heritage Society of Providence, Rhode Island (1975-1985). Stewart has served as president of the African American Museums Association, president of the Coalition of African American Organizations in Philadelphia, visiting scholar at Brown University in Afro-American Studies, trustee of the Rhode Island Historical Society and Brown University Rites and Reason, and chairperson of the Rhode Island State Council for the Arts. She is also the author of publications including *Blacks in Tourism* and *Roots and Remedies: Afro-American Folk Medicines in Rhode Island.*

Marcia White is acting chairperson of the American Museum of Natural History's Education Department. She began her career at the museum in 1977, and has held the positions of coordinator for community programs, manager for teaching programs and assistant chairperson for teaching programs in the Education Department. Before coming to the American Museum of Natural History, she worked as a manager at The Children's Museum, Boston. White has served as a reviewer and panelist for the New York State Council on the Arts, New York Council for the Humanities and the Massachusetts Council on the Arts. She earned a B.A. from Simmons College in Boston and received a certificate in special events marketing from New York University in 1993.

Acknowledgments

In 1985 the National Endowment for the Arts awarded me a Museum Fellowship that allowed me to take a six-month sabbatical from my job as director, exhibit center at The Children's Museum, Boston and move to England to write and reflect on what had occurred in 1979 when the museum moved to its downtown location. The program and the endowment itself serve as the catalyst for this project.

During that time in England, I was granted reading privileges at the library of the London Business School where for the first time I read management literature that allowed me to understand that museum administrators were not alone.

My chapter, "Moving the Museum," resulted from that six months of work and began its independent journey as an "underground best seller," passing from hand to hand in many generations of photocopied manuscript.

The original chapter was commented on by many Children's Museum colleagues and friends—Eleanor Chin, Signe Hanson, Aylette Jenness, Janet Kamien, Suzanne LeBlanc, Dorothy Merriell and Patricia Steuart—who read patiently and thoughtfully. Chief among the then Children's Museum staff, I would like to thank Ann Tribble Butterfield, who edited version after version of my chapter and who believed that, in fact, one *could* teach a dyslexic to write.

During the ensuing 10 years between the completion of the original chapter and this book, each of my assistants (Marylou Abrigo, Juanita Sayles and Lisa Watt) kept the project alive by reformatting or re-editing the document into ever new software and then sending out new versions upon request. Lysa Kless kept the book on track while helping to open the United States Holocaust Memorial Museum at the same time. I owe her a special debt of gratitude.

After returning from England, rather than completing the book, I went from one start-up museum project to another, becoming a veteran of professional trauma. Tom Freudenheim, Michael Spock, Jeshajahu Weinberg and Richard West, Jr., my bosses and work partners during those years, each had enough faith to allow me to participate in the work of starting, opening or moving their museum or project. I am grateful for their trust and for their friendship. I wish to thank all the staff who supported the work we did together to make dreams into realizations.

In 1993, the American Association of Museums agreed to publish this book. I am grateful to Ed Able, president and CEO of AAM, for his confidence, and most especially to John Strand, director of publications, and his staff—Associate Editor Susannah Cassedy O'Donnell and Design and Production Manager Polly Franchine—for working with each author in a thoughtful and careful editing process.

In 1993 many colleagues answered the request for authors that appeared in AAM's monthly newsletter *Aviso* and volunteered to write about their experiences. I would like to thank all those whose chapters appear here and those who volunteered but were not chosen. The authors were willing to carve time out of their ongoing tasks and help their colleagues by telling their own stories.

Finally, I would like to thank my children, who encourage me, and my life partner Dean Anderson, who reads all my writings and makes sure the words match my thoughts. Without his kindness and support I would not endeavor to write at all.

Elaine Heumann Gurian
April 1995

Preface

Elaine Heumann Gurian

In the course of any museum's history, events that cause significant change inevitably happen. When they do, we as administrators should not be surprised that they affect staff in profound ways.

This book is written as a source of company and comfort for everyone who works in museums. However, it is written expressly from the administrator's point of view and for those members of staff who can effect change. The authors in this volume of case studies write in two separate but intertwined voices: that of staff, to which they belong, and that of managers, those who were in a position to affect the course of events.

It is the authors' wish that administrators, armed with the experience of others, will go forth with renewed energy to face the challenges posed by change and mitigate the trauma felt by their colleagues, while also taking care of their own beleaguered and often lonely selves. I hope that this book will prove helpful by portraying reliable examples of administrative action and staff reaction, and thereby encourage appropriately preventive and continuous care.

This book aims to present information that is a step up from the "how-to" manual and a step down from a theoretical academic treatise: a usable book for busy people. The museum case studies contained in this volume are about specific events written by the participants who held major management positions at the time. In each case the initial trauma described took place at least 18 months previously. The time elapsed allowed the writers to gain perspective on their own feelings and the feelings of the staff as well.

The chapters have been organized into categories that relate to the primary source of the trauma itself. Obviously there are many more museum events that cause staff distress, and most changes have multiple causes and outcomes. However, the histories of all museums contain predictably painful events that affect staff profoundly, and it is from these that the case studies were chosen.

What are some of the major changes that can become traumatic events in the life of an institution and its staff? In the world of museums, these can be divided into categories that include:

The Building

Opening a new building or new museum

Construction of any kind

Unhealthful work environment causing staff illness

Physical damage to the building caused by a natural or man-made disaster

Staff

Death of the director or staff member

Turnover of director

Professionalizing a volunteer institution and hiring the first paid director

Organized staff discontent

Illegal/actionable behavior on part of staff or director

Governance

Budget cuts and/or staff layoffs

Merging two institutions

Closing the museum

Theft of collections objects

Cancellation of capital improvements or expansion plans

Refocusing or changing the mission

Pressure to cancel or alter exhibition content

The situations written about in this book are emblematic enough to be useful to anyone who is either on the verge or in the midst of a stressful museum change. I hope that the reader will find that these case studies when taken as a whole illustrate common predictable reactions and offer strategies that help administrators and staff deal effectively with significant change.

•

Collectively, these chapters suggest some important lessons for museum professionals. These include:

Staff will be affected by any significant change, and the effects will continue over a long period of time.

A group may go through a collective emotional grieving process in the same way individuals do.

This patterned process may not be apparent to the staff, leaving individuals blaming themselves or thinking they are the only ones suffering. Therefore, administrators need to be proactive and encourage group understanding of the process.

One result of major change will be discomfort no matter what we do. There is no such thing as a "traumaless trauma." However, it is our responsibility as managers to forecast the stages, prepare the staff and ameliorate the situation whenever possible.

Most important, this attention to staff discomfort *is* our work. It is neither an interruption nor an intrusion.

Since we as administrators are also affected by events, we must be introspective enough to differentiate our needs from those of our staff. If we are personally uncomfortable with feelings expressed within the context of work, we need to learn a management style that will help the staff cope with and ultimately survive the painful situation. Because management is a lonely business, we may need our own external support system of colleagues and professionals in order to do that.

The consequences of *not* helping our staff through a sustained, profound change may be an exacerbation of disturbances within the staff and, ultimately, disruption of work.

•

This is a book about collective, not individual, stress, and about institutional, not personal, coping mechanisms. Yet the literature on individual stress in the workplace may provide interesting insights for us.

Non-participation at work (the primary indicator of individual job stress) can be seen in "overall poor physical health, escapist drinking, depressed mood, low self-esteem, low life satisfaction, low job satisfaction, low motivation at work, intention to leave one's job and absenteeism from work."[1]

I postulate that such unremitting and untreated stress within an organization will produce a collective response within 18 months. The following, by extrapolation of individual work stress symptoms, might be indicators that unrelieved group stressors are present:

Excessive employee illness or absences

Large number of individual upheavals, such as marital separation, divorce, excessive drinking, etc.

Collective depression and lethargy resulting in work slowdown

Interest in grumbling, rumors and scapegoating so consuming that it interferes with output

Agitation, secret meetings, petitions, strikes or work stoppages

Staff complaints to board members

Unanticipated and seemingly inordinate staff turnover

•

Because change has emotional consequence for staff, the premise of this book is that management has a responsibility to pay attention to the psychological and emotional well-being of their staff and themselves. Much management literature praises the creation of "company culture" and other approaches to holistic management methods. That literature has suggested that staff-supportive management with attendant internal structures of support tends to create more employee satisfaction, commitment and better job performance. The argument, at base, is that being supportive is also being efficient.

It is, therefore, in our best interests to pay attention to the feelings, expressions of disgruntlement and suggestions for improvements offered by our team. We need to collect enough data to distinguish between the individual who has an unrelated gripe and those who are spokespersons for the many with legitimate expressions of dissatisfaction. Paying attention, hearing accurately, suggesting solutions and being forthright and timely with information—even negative information—may lead to a diminution of symptoms interfering with work and allow workers to concentrate better on quality performance.

It is my experience that staff continue optimistically to face difficulties no matter how severe and to suggest positive solutions so long as they feel they:

are being dealt with honestly

have access to both good and bad, but timely information

are respected and recognized for their production and devotion

believe that non-performance is dealt with consistently and fairly

understand the mission and objectives of the organization

believe that leaders are advocating on behalf of the staff

trust management is doing whatever it can to regain control of the situation.

•

Without all or most of these ingredients in place, sometime between 12 and 18 months following significant change, staff will begin to organize against management, and serious and systematized disruption can be expected.

Even if impaired work performance were not the outcome of unabated staff stress, I would proffer another, and perhaps better reason to pay attention to staff needs. If our work in museums is evidence of our collective commitment to enhancing the quality of life for society, then we must be attentive to maintaining a high quality of life for our work community. If we would not allow our biological family to mourn a death without our support, why should we expect to do less for our work family?

A note of caution: if as managers our desire to lead is not held in check, we risk encouraging emotional responses when individuals may not want or need them. We cannot order our staff to "mourn now because it will be good for us." As managers we must constantly struggle between over- and under-directing.

The following case studies will reflect this struggle. All "cures" need not be generated by the "bosses." The staff has a role in healing itself, and can provide significant leadership in suggesting what might be needed. If given an opportunity to express it, they have some perspective and care for the manager's pain, as well.

The case studies presented and the reflections and recommendations made are in the service of helping others. They are not intended to expose anyone's lack of skill or judgment. Yet seeing how mistakes are made is necessary if we are to distinguish unavoidable strain from that which could be prevented in our own futures. As incorrect as some of our decisions may now appear in retrospect, we may at least console ourselves with the knowledge that we did the best we could at the time. These recountings are used primarily to orient the reader and explain the context in which staff responded. The writers of the individual case studies sometimes name names. The chapters are intentionally particularized in order to allow the author to focus on his or her own story rather than produce a more generic narrative.

Finally, it is our collective hope that this volume can serve our colleagues and help create a more supportive museum workplace.

1. Cary Cooper, "Work Stress," *Psychology at Work*, ed. Peter B. Warr (Middlesex, England: Penguin Books, Ltd.: 1978), p. 286.

Introduction

Rina Bar-Lev Elieli and Laurence J. Gould

This book is a collection of articles chronicling the changes that have taken place in different museums throughout the United States. These were changes that brought with them a feeling that in their wake nothing would be the same again—changes that left scars of pain and discontent in the organization's memory, even though they may have led to development, both directly and indirectly. The word trauma appears in the title of the book, as if to suggest that every change occurring in the museum world is accompanied by these disturbing feelings associated with the phenomenon of trauma. The question that always presents itself in a traumatic situation is: Will there be some development that will enable the organization to weather the difficult crisis, or will the crisis lead to an overall breakdown?

What is the connection between the word "trauma" and the unique nature of museums as institutions in the community? Or is the fear of trauma inherent in every process of change in every organization?

Museums are institutions with an extremely important function within every community in which they are found. They are institutions that preserve memory, that document the development of the specific community and of the world with all its diverse secrets. They are the collective memory of a civilization and its culture, and thus they symbolize succession and continuity. They identify the community within which they operate as a part of the total span of the universe. They emphasize the similarity and divergence among different communities, those closer and those farther away. To one extent or another, they constitute an interactive element between the community and its roots, between it and other communities, and act as an integrative element within the community.

The question of the uniqueness of the museum as an institution in the community runs like a thread throughout all the articles in this book. It is not explicitly addressed because the articles do not deal with this question. They relate a segment of transition in the course of the museum's life, an excerpt from the museum's history. We, the writers of this introduction, who come from a different discipline—psychology—that deals with the uniqueness of entities in the life of the psyche and the life of the society, find it difficult to avoid asking this question about the unique place of the museum in the community. To this question, we will attempt to offer an answer that inevitably can only be partial. It will, however, provide an additional vantage point, an additional context that welds all the stories in this volume into a totality that carries an additional meaning.

A museum is an institution that allows a community to look at itself. This function of self-observation—of review—is like taking a new look into a mirror. The image reflected in the mirror provides an overall picture of what is in the inventory of the culture, in the storehouse of memories. What is there? How do we look? What do we lack that others have? How do others see us? What are our plans for the future? Like any self-observation that makes us pause in our everyday activity and adopt the stance of a spectator from the inside and the outside simultaneously, a visit to a museum takes place during a break in the flow of daily life. A museum visit is a time out from the current of routine activity, in order to look, to absorb, to assimilate and to learn. We are carried by an introspective current at a museum. Adults usually engage in this activity on their own, as a couple or in a small group, while children participate on a more social group level, visiting the museum with their families or on school trips.

It is the very existence of museums, along with the special activity of every individual in every age group during their visit to the museum, that enable the community to take an overall look at itself. This function of self-observation is of course adjunct to all the traditional functions assigned to museums, in particular education and the broadening of knowledge.

From this standpoint, a museum is a sort of meta-institution that enables the community to address itself and other communities from two points of view simultaneously. The first is the inner, core viewpoint of essence: Who are we? The second is an external viewpoint to the cycle: how we look to others.

A good illustration of this would be a Native American from the northwestern United States visiting an exhibition of Italian Renaissance art at a Seattle museum. The question of comparison, similarity and divergence is after all a central part of every observation. Indeed, that museum in Seattle may at the same time mount an exhibition on the ritual ceremonies of Native Americans in the Northwest, and on the floor above show its permanent collection of art from peoples all over the globe.

This function within the community is undoubtedly very vital. It may not seem to be, since people go to museums only in their leisure time or when there is something new and important to see. As an institution in the community, the museum organizes, stabilizes and assimilates the story of the existence of the universe into the fabric of everyday life. This is hardly self-evident when one considers that museums display exhibits to the public that rarely deal with the daily life of the present at all, but with things from the past. The link to our own time is constantly preserved in the perception and imagination of the visitor, the spectator.

There is an air of sanctity in every museum, that can be—and perhaps should be—mixed with the profane. This mixture gives humanity the dimension of being everyone's province. Belonging to the human species takes on the coloration of a real experience. The distant comes closer, the close and the familiar also acquire greater value and importance, and from the close-by one can move farther away in order to get a new angle of observation. Every individual feels part of this complex fabric.

We realize that this function of the museum in the community is not an obvious one. It is not something we sense at each and every moment. We have to stop and think about this multitude of meanings. It is an unconscious function, just as other institutions in the community have functions that are beyond the explicit objective assigned to them, just as many of our thoughts and many of the processes occurring inside us are not conscious. For example, we become conscious of our breathing only when it is disturbed, and then this awareness is accompanied by a strong sense of anxiety. Institutions that preserve and transmit civilization are like the rhythmic breaths of a living entity. Museums protect the healthy rhythm of life—the backbone of culture. The public, as a rule, takes these institutions for granted. Only those charged with maintaining and operating them will react to any threat to their well-being with great anxiety usually reserved for situations in which one feels the threat of annihilation. Indeed, what is involved here is the safeguarding of civilization. Any threat to fulfilling this role is apt to be experienced as an incurable trauma. How is someone responsible for preserving continuity supposed to carry out this duty and undergo self-transformations at the same time? This is a dilemma that is liable to be experienced as trauma.

This book deals with the everyday, with the "profane," even though the events it describes were experienced by the narrators of the stories and by other staff members of the museum as difficult and painful episodes in the development of the organization, and which aroused disturbing questions about the continued existence of the museums. These are descriptions of events that could take place in any organization. The everyday here defines the museum as an organization that must be properly run while providing a service to its community.

Although the function of museums in the community touches upon the sanctity of essences, in the daily conduct of their work they are like all organizations. They are run by individuals amalgamated into an organization that is more than the sum of its parts. The role of this organization and its various staffs is to achieve the aims set forth by its overall objective. And the realization of these aims, as sanctified as they may be, involves the hard daily work of people—so difficult and demanding that they often forget the sanctity of their mission.

All of the events described in this volume were recounted and recorded by people holding key positions at their museums. Their stories clearly reveal a high degree of dedication to their work, the organization itself, staff and management, as well as to the museum's community. They also reveal an affinity to the social mission of preserving civilization for the community. It is abundantly obvious that the writers do not credit themselves with such qualities. This is apparently due to their modesty, but also to the perspective from which they are writing. This is a viewpoint that stems from the hard work of coping with the changes, crises and traumas that constantly confront them in daily life and jeopardize their ability to fulfill their objective.

All of the events related in the book originate in the normal flow of life, in the processes of development and in the stumbling blocks that interrupt this flow. In using the phrase "the normal flow of life," we by no means intend to underestimate the difficulties these organizations confront as they develop. These struggles are exacerbated when institutions cope with special events requiring them to mobilize resources from within the system in order to emerge from them as whole as possible and to return to the normal routine, enriched and even stronger. The life of every organization making progress is replete with transitions and changes.

Like a photograph album, this collection portrays events on a continuum in which there is a special stress on events characterized by change. In the different chapters, there is particular reference to what existed before the event and what occurred during the particular events. But there are few descriptions of a return to routine. The stories almost always end with what is so difficult to see during a crisis—the future. Every organization acquires the ability to grasp the future by drawing on the reservoir of its developmental strengths. It is the ability to look at the future during the present situation of numerous difficulties—a situation considered hopeless—that makes reorganization possible. During a crisis it is hard to see the routine that will follow. Often the feeling is so stifling, so deeply felt as an "end of the world" experience, that the horizon is invisible.

In the title of the book, "trauma" unifies all the case studies. There is an assumption here that every event of change is traumatic, that every event of change is like a wound inflicted by an element that upsets the existing balance and whose penetration is experienced as violent. The task of organizing after this injury is so enormously difficult that it is sensed as impossible. It is still necessary to identify the source of this penetrating and injurious element. Does it come from outside the system or from within? Is it a part of development or is it a force obstructing growth and development?

How are other concepts—development, stages of transition, change, crisis, trauma, the return to routine—interrelated? These can be viewed as concepts on one cognitive continuum. Their common denominator is the fact that they constitute markers of change in the annals of an institution. All these concepts deal with the metamorphoses of situations, but they describe different gradations of pain and suffering involved in the fact of change itself. These concepts are central to the descriptions of the events recorded in this book.

According to J. Laplanche and B. Pontalis (1980) in *The Language of Psychoanalysis* (translated by Donald Nicholson-Smith, London: The Hogarth Press and The Institute of Psycho-Analysis), (psychical) trauma is:

> An event in the subject's life defined by its intensity, by the subject's incapacity to respond adequately to it, and by the upheaval and long-lasting effects that it brings about in the psychical organization. . . . The trauma is characterized by an influx of excitation that is excessive by the standard of the subject's tolerance and capacity to master such excitations and work them out psychically. It is a term that has long been used in medicine and surgery. It generally means any injury where the skin is broken as a consequence of external violence, and the effects of such an injury upon the organism as a whole. In adopting the term, psychoanalysis carries the three ideas implicit in it over onto the psychical level: the idea of a violent shock, the idea of a wound and the idea of consequences affecting the whole organization. (p. 465-466)

This definition of trauma within the context of an individual can also be applied to the realm of an organization and/or group. A general organizational concept is implicit in the term "trauma" itself. One part is wounded and impaired and the entire system reacts by expressing the difficulty of organizing.

There is a profound understanding among psychoanalysts that every change by virtue of being change is accompanied by pain and arises from pain. This is pain associated with the loss of the previous moment, the loss of something known, familiar and close, something normal. It is the loss of the habitual. A new situation, insofar as we can imagine, describe or plan it, still remains something that has not yet been experienced in external reality. No matter how prepared we are, no matter how much we have developed our ability to foresee the future, there is still considerable room left for the unknown, for surprise. Not to mention unplanned, unanticipated, sudden situations, for which there is no advance preparation. These situations may be experienced as a crisis, even as a trauma, even if in the final analysis they will lead to changes for the better. When is a change considered a trauma, particularly in an institution like a museum whose objective is to preserve permanence and memory? In such an organization, every change will seem traumatic.

In the flow of life, everything can be seen as transitory. The concepts of permanence and continuity, which are so important, take on added significance because every moment we have to adjust to a new situation. It is an awareness of this flow that enables individuals as well as organizations to see themselves living, working and functioning within a transitional space in which change and transition are an essential part of reality. The ability to manage this "transitionality" and to conduct one's life from within it is of decisive importance in attaining the flexibility needed for growth and development. Knowing that there are mechanisms available that are strong, resistant, flexible and possessed of creative forces, helps individuals and organizations cope with crisis.

A crisis situation leads to an inevitable result that calls for some remedial action to prevent further deterioration. It calls for emergency mobilization. In the normal, daily, routine course of life, a system develops a sense of stability vital to the functions it has to perform. There is a sense of balance in which the everyday modes of coping are adaptive, familiar, suitable and reliable. This sense of stability is a part of taking into account normal changes that occur, and can sometimes counteract the need to continually adapt to this "transitionality." To avoid frequently sensing change, we can develop an illusion of permanence and non-change. This illusion may be illustrated by the example of a line. We know that a continuous line is composed of a series of dots. We can perceive each dot separately and home in on it for a long time, or we can perceive the line as a flowing continuum. Homing in on only one dot gives us the sense that it is the sole existing dot, like a solitary island in mid-ocean from which you cannot see any other island. Is there an adaptive way to grasp the separate dots and the linear flow at the same time?

When particularly difficult problems arise, the organization mobilizes the coping mechanisms it knows—those that have worked well in previous situations. A crisis is perceived when the system feels it is facing an obstacle preventing it from realizing one of its important, vital aims, an obstacle that cannot be overcome and resolved through a normal way of coping. These situations are accompanied by trying emotional difficulties that center on issues of forces, strength, resistance and the ability of the organization and its leaders to cope. Frequently, these situations are accompanied by a decline in confidence in the organization's leadership.

The leadership of the organization—whether it is a group or an individual—finds itself on the boundary between the organization and the crisis. Everyone's eyes are on the leaders. They are the ones who are supposed to know how to lead the organization out of the crisis. They are supposed to hold the key to the organization's reservoir of strength and resources. They are the guardians of continuity and tradition, of knowledge and of the right path. From this position on the border between the organization and the environment, the leaders are supposed to navigate the way out of the crisis to the solution. Each of the articles in the book emphasizes the role of the leader as the one who ought to be capable of looking inward and outward at the same time. A leader must look inward to what is happening to the people, put his finger on the pulse of the organization, sense the discontent of the people in it, and know what will make them feel good. At the same time, he must look outward, seeing the road leading to the realization of the objective. The objective may be realized by correctly safeguarding the various roles of the people and departments in the organization and by conducting appropriate negotiations with outside factors.

The crisis generally brings in its wake a period marked by disorganization and confusion, a general sense of ineffectiveness, in particular in relation to the specific solution of the crisis. That same emergency situation—a special mobilization of the system around the issues of survival—if it endures for a long time, will cause feelings of erosion, infirmity and enervation. People in the system long to return to the previous familiar routine. The knowledge that there is no going back to the point of departure, other than by paying the price of ignoring reality, is very painful. Processes of development exist throughout this time in the personal, as well as in the interpersonal and intersystemic worlds. Ignoring these processes is tantamount to ignoring reality. The naive view of a return to the routine will bring with it the childish wish to go back to the point of departure, thus canceling out the trauma. The mature view will take into account the changes and the inner place that has to be created in order to go about the task of mourning. This task involves the emotional working through of the sorrow over what previously existed, the loss, and the ability to turn this loss into a part of the inner world, the world of memories, part of the culture, of the symbolic reality.

The crisis situation also arouses anxiety about the existence of the individual in the system. Every change in an organization, in its institutions, in the definition of its tasks, constitutes a threat to the security of the individual. The place of the individual is no longer as safe as it was before. A change in the system often means a change in personnel. This mix of the organization's and the individual's anxieties makes it difficult to find a good enough formula for organizing with confidence in the future.

The ordeals of an organization are experienced in their totality by the organization as a whole. All of the organization's employees, or the various staffs and departments as a subgroup of the organization, carry with them a picture, an experience, an impression and story of the event from their vantage point in the organization. This vantage point is created by the formal and informal, conscious and unconscious role of those individuals or sub-groups in the organization's life. Museums, like all organizations, differ from one another. They may undergo similar processes that are described in similar terms, but they are different. This variance is palpably felt when one enters an institution, and immediately and inexplicably senses the special atmosphere of the place, just as on entering different people's houses, the visitor encounters the quintessence of each home. Our encounter with organizations is also described in words we would use to describe individuals. There are many points of similarity, but there are also many points of disparity.

One of the crisis situations depicted in the book is the move of a museum from one home to another. The move to a different building, albeit a more beautiful, larger, more suitable one, is always a source of stress. A change of domicile is known to be a common source of feelings of depression and stress. The crisis in this case, among both individuals and organizations, calls for reorganization on all levels of existence. It is necessary to recreate the inner home, to examine the new inner atmosphere that is created in the new home, to search for the previous atmosphere that may have disappeared and is still bound up with feelings and identities that belonged to the previous home. A new external organization, which strongly influences feelings of internal orientation, has to take place too.

By connecting all these diverse points of view of individuals and sub-groups in the organization, we will get the full story, to the extent that that is at all possible. When all is said and done, every story is, by its very nature, a kind of interpretation. Nonetheless, it is possible to use this ideal opportunity to write the story in full. This will be a story of what previously existed. This will be the story that will be told after the return to normal, after the event, or after the period of crisis—in other words, the story that will be told from a point further removed in time, from the place where memories—the history—are recounted.

Transmitting things from a different point in time is actually the function of museums. As soon as objects are put on display in a museum, they become the "permanent," and the museum becomes that which preserves permanence. Hence, any impairment of this possibility to preserve the continuity of transmitting things will be experienced by those charged with this task as endangering their ability to fulfill it, and as threatening the existence of the heritage. In our time, the task of guarding the flame, the glowing ember, has been entrusted to those who preserve the civilization. Any possibility that this flame may die out is so distressing a trauma one can hardly imagine a panacea for it.

Part One

The Building

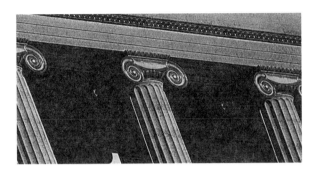

Moving the Museum

The Children's Museum, Boston

Elaine Heumann Gurian

Introduction

I came to the The Children's Museum (TCM) in 1971 to become Exhibit Center director and part of a management team of three division directors who worked under Michael Spock, the museum's director. Under unusual arrangements, I was responsible for the planning, designing and building of exhibitions as well as the hiring, training and, if need be, the disciplining of the interpretative and operations staff. The division directors had autonomy in their own areas, designed their own staffing systems and created and managed their own budgets. Each week the division directors (known as the managers) met together with Mike to deal with issues that were museum-wide. Our agreement to a joint policy was crafted with patience and by consensus. There was never a vote taken and rarely was a decision imposed by the director. The members of the management group respected and trusted each other.

The Children's Museum under Michael Spock was known for its humanistic, familial tone. Our style was friendly and informal. For most of the staff, the museum work was part of their creative life. This made us a cohesive organization filled with an almost nationalistic fervor. In some ways, we were a unique museum.

The question then arises: Is the following experience about physically moving The Children's Museum so idiosyncratic that it is of little use to anyone else? I have questioned a small sample of staff from other institutions who have been involved in a move or a building expansion, and their responses have mirrored our own in form, though they were different in detail. I believe that there were important lessons learned in our case that can be of real benefit to others.

This, then, is an attempt to reflect on our particular move, some 15 years after the opening of The Children's Museum at Museum Wharf, in order to be helpful to readers who may find themselves in similar situations.

Background

On July 1, 1979, The Children's Museum opened in its new home on the waterfront in downtown Boston. Since its inception in 1913, the museum had always been located in the more suburban Jamaica Plain. One hundred eighty thousand visitors annually tried to cram into 7,000 square feet of public space At peak times there was often an hour's wait to get into the Exhibit Center. We were unable to accommodate a larger audience and faced rising staff costs. Our decision to move was prompted by economic necessity. We decided to move and grow rather than to stay and suffocate.

Studies projected our potential market at between 400,000 and 600,000 annual visitors if we located ourselves more centrally, close to public transportation and in a more ethnically neutral area. Armed with this information and with the commitment of the museum's board, the move took place after nearly 10 years of planning, primarily by Michael Spock. He looked at more than 15 sites, commissioned a detailed report on four of them, and conducted a full-scale feasibility study on two.

During the previous three-and-a-half years (1975-1979), The Children's Museum simultaneously ran a capital campaign, expanded the Resource Center, and planned, tried-out, built, stored and finally installed new exhibits. We closed our previous site to the public for only 10 weeks, packed, moved staff (with the exception of the collections and the design and production studio, which we moved later), and we opened at the beginning of our busiest season, the summer of 1979. We started with nine separate opening events.

With this move to Boston's rejuvenated waterfront, our public space increased from 7,000 to 18,000 square feet and our attendance went from 180,000 to 470,000 in the first year. Ten thousand people went to the opening parties, and by the end of the first 12 weeks, 180,000 visitors came, the same number we served during the entire previous year.

The staff was both proud and exhausted. It was primarily the staff that accomplished this move, focusing on the external task but at the same time experiencing a range of feelings.

The following is a recounting of the events and the attendant patterns of staff behavior for the years preceding opening (primarily 1976-1979) and for the first operating year (July 1979-July 1980) as seen through the eyes of the director of the Exhibit Center.

Staff Involvement in the Planning Process

Planning for the museum began in 1974 with both the senior management and the board committed to relocation. The staff was invited to go on a retreat held at a rural inn. Collectively, they suggested goals for the museum and the program that would result and listed their needs for individual work space. The retreat was hard work done in an informal atmosphere. It became a cohesive experience that remained as an island of idealism and optimism throughout the difficult months that followed. Each individual was asked to complete a workbook for use later by the planners. Some thought the workbook was impractical, too casual in tone and filled with dreams. It subsequently proved useful as a reference tool. It was sometimes even prophetic.

At the same time, some members of the staff and board were invited by Michael Spock to form the program committee that was charged with formulating the future program of the museum and its space implications. The committee met monthly and issued memos that were circulated among all staff for consideration and comment. The process, though vague and only occasionally interesting, was, in retrospect, useful. Meeting every month with key staff and board members helped synthesize collective thinking and make it more practical. The time devoted to the process allowed the entire staff to understand and then to "buy in" to a collective dream. The program committee document, when finished and circulated, allowed staff to make independent but compatible decisions within their own spheres.

Over the next two years (1974-1976), there were many other meetings with the whole staff and specialized groups. Lists were made of everything from names of potential co-tenants to desirable paint colors. Staff from the divisions were not used to looking at overall museum issues and none of us had learned how the planning process worked. Sometimes the meetings seemed endlessly repetitious and filled with wishful thinking, and kept us from what we thought of as our primary work, running the existing public facility.

There came a time for me and many of my co-workers when we were "planned out." Moving seemed remote, irrelevant and often unreal. From that point on, either we did not go to planning meetings or we went with desultory interest and a great deal of skepticism. Our churlishness lasted a long time (1975-1977) and our attitude changed only when we began to feel that at last the move was imminent. Despite our irritation, our skill in planning improved and we became more useful members of the team in spite of ourselves.

Getting Ready

We bought our new building in 1975, four years before we opened. We took all the staff to see the old wool warehouse in a section of Boston that had not yet been rediscovered. We arrived on a cold and gloomy day in rented school buses. There are photos to record that event and one can see how the staff divided between the excited and the totally disbelieving.

The staff understood very quickly that the process of renovation was one in which we did not have expertise. It became essential for us to rely on outside experts and our director for guidance. We were used to relying primarily on ourselves and we expressed hesitancy and some distrust working with "strangers." We absorbed some of the "experts" and made them into family and heroes. Some, however, became the "enemy" and the externalized lightning rods of our anger. Because so much of the future appeared murky and blind faith was sometimes the only way forward, our trust in Mike was fortunately well founded. By 1975 he had been at the museum for 13 years and was a known quantity who was admired and respected.

The project seemed more or less real to us depending on how much it affected our daily work at any given moment. Some of the serious hurdles seemed quite remote, like putting the bank funding package together. Some seemed quite immediate, like a threatened strike by the union construction workers against the open-shop policy.

The fund-raising staff worked in a trailer at the wharf site for two years. For them, the new museum was more real than our operation in Jamaica Plain and they viewed the rest of the staff as interlopers. Mike gave up his desk in Jamaica Plain and appeared there once a week to occupy a table in a meeting room. With all the attention of the senior staff focused downtown, the staff entrusted with running the "old" museum began to feel devalued and forgotten. They took on a certain martyred quality.

During the two years before we opened, staff were experiencing waves of feelings that ranged from optimism to petulance. This seemed to change daily. One staff member entered into a phase of secession. She decided that whatever swirled around her, she would remain unaffected because emotionally she was no longer there—she was in a mythical Miami. She continued to do her daily work effectively but took no part in anything that had to do with moving. Although all of us could have profited by taking a lesson from her and paying a little less attention to our own anxiety, we could not have condoned the actions of many staff members like her. In reality, she left us to do all the organization required for the move. But she was a beloved staff member, and no one really resented her. On the day we moved, she came with us and remained an important member of the staff.

The Effect of Installation on the Design and Production Staff

The building renovators were supposed to produce finished exhibition space ready for installation by January for the July opening. Because of threatened strikes and construction delays beyond our control, we never had any totally finished space up to and including opening day. Further, because our production team was not unionized, we were advised not to let them install when the construction was going on for fear that the unions would bring the entire project to a halt.

The design and production (D&P) staff had built exhibits continuously for 18 months. The exhibits were stored everywhere including a rented truck container on the grounds. We promised D&P clean, finished space ready for exhibition installation beginning January 1st. They prepared an installation and construction schedule that was achievable because it was phased. They grew understandably anxious as each new day went by without their being allowed to begin. As February and March went by they became very angry at me, Mike and the construction team for having failed to deliver on our promised schedule. Their good will for the project was diminished and their faith in me as their leader was at a low ebb. D&P leadership thought that they would be personally blamed when (no longer if) the installation was not completed on time, because we, the museum staff, would collectively fail to remember the construction hold-ups and would assume either poor planning or incompetence on their part. Their professional pride and reputations were at stake. Feelings of anger and frustration ran understandably high. I felt impotent and took to a series of "raised voice" sessions with the construction manager—to no avail.

Thus, 10 weeks before the opening, I understood that to install the exhibits (and possibly still open on time), we would just have to work with the construction going on around us and the construction workers still in the building. From then on, we referred to "The Christopher Columbus theory of installation" and used the motto "All land we conquer is ours!" Every day we loaded finished exhibitions into a truck and drove to the unsecured, under-construction space and installed them.

The building construction crew were not used to working side by side with museum carpenters who included women and pony-tailed men. Some of our carpenters had chosen to work at the museum because it suited them better than traditional construction jobs and they were hostile to the construction milieu. Some construction workers greeted the museum installers with leers and name-calling. The women carpenters got alternately militant and conciliatory, with many conversations arising about capitulating and changing their uniform from the jeans and T-shirts that all carpenters wear to something less revealing.

However, what started out as hostility eventually ended in mutual respect when each side came to appreciate the real skill the others brought to their work. They began to know each other's names and to understand that each side was interested in a museum for children. Not surprisingly, each side had to confront and let go of stereotypes in order ultimately to work well together.

The Effect of Collections Installations on Curators

We planned to install museum collections in phases, as well. In our modest planning space known as the "war room," schedules showed dates that announced the end of each exhibit installation and the beginning of the collection installation. To make up for lost time, we had to install collections and exhibits simultaneously. This was not only a conservational compromise, but in this process the collections were potentially insecure. The building was wide open, and authorized and unauthorized workers were everywhere. We had expected to have very few cases open at any one time so we could monitor them closely. Instead, we installed as fast as we could and hired unbudgeted security officers (really college kids on summer holiday) to sit by each case until it was closed, to protect the objects from theft.

The curators had always been responsible for the state and security of the collections. They had nurtured them and now they were being told to install under conditions that appeared to be neither safe nor secure and included paint fumes and construction dust. Furthermore, the curators were being told to compromise their professional standards by people they liked and trusted. They were understandably upset. We, the supervisors, were in emotional upheaval as well, as we tried to decide if our standards could be temporarily lowered. All of us tried to invent systems that would let curators install with some measure of comfort while continuing to move the project forward. We compromised by commandeering a room, setting it up exclusively for collections. There was space enough to lay out cases prior to installation and there were temporary but appropriate security systems. This meant diverting the computer personnel from working on their permanent installation, which caused them to ruin their schedule, as well. It took them more than a year to recover from this delay. Every change caused more and more staff to be faced with tasks that seemed impossible to complete as the deadline fast approached.

The Effect of Unfinished Offices on Staff

The office space construction was not completed either, but for a different reason. In our planning, the management had agreed to maximize our income by using our first capital funds to open as much exhibition and public space as we could afford. We would delay the building of finished space for offices until the completion of the second capital campaign and live collectively within the unimproved space for the subsequent six years. While the staff understood the reasons for this, it meant that people were moving from finished, though makeshift offices in Jamaica Plain to unfinished, sometimes unheated camping-out spaces at Museum Wharf—a clear step down in some cases.

The TCM staff completed the move with remarkable good humor, working very hard to get the opening ready. They did not focus on their offices or understand what these would ultimately look like because every space was knee-deep in packing cases. It would be later, after the opening, that the reality of living in the uncomfortable office situation would add to the built-up anger.

Managers

During the final 10 weeks we all often felt optimistic, confident and encouraged. It was an exciting time.

Alternatively, with the rush to open, managers also felt afraid that their tasks would not be done on time and they would appear incompetent, while still having to be supportive of others. We would often seek each other out, close the door and emotionally reveal our anxieties. The need for peer support during these times was critical, not so much for substantive advice as for real succor.

Two weeks before the new site opened, Michael Spock and I found that most of the decisions for which we were responsible had been made, and that we were virtually out of work. There was no "directing" needed now. Only physical work remained to be done. We applied to the construction crew for manual work and were accepted. We both arrived daily in work clothes, eager to be included. We would slip out of the roles only occasionally and only when a decision was needed that forced us to assume our old positions. I don't think the crew knew how grateful we were. Sitting by without sufficient work during this stressful time would have been impossible. Because the staff was used to a matrix form of decision making, they did not have any trouble giving us orders and, most of the time, we clearly understood that we worked for them.

The "charrette" associated with exhibition installations, like theater openings, bonds people. The pressure of installation, while stressful, was relieved by rituals, practical jokes, silly gags and late-night pizzas. It was a time filled with private language that made it difficult for anyone other than the initiated to break in. This behavior helped us get through the war. However, it had the attendant difficulty of creating a "them and us" situation. When the shop was later moved to a separate location, it set D&P apart from the rest of the staff for a long time.

Two days before we opened we found that, miraculously, we had completed construction on time and under budget, with only finishing touches left to do. On that day, every content specialist visited me to tell me with certainty that all the other exhibits were better than his or hers and it was clearly my fault. By each one in turn, I was accused of favoritism for someone else.

On that same day, the construction part of D&P declared that they would no longer work for their supervisor and that they wanted him fired. They revealed that they had been watching him carefully, noting his seeming insensitivity, but had not wanted to come to me until the job was finished. During the preceding weeks, unknown to me, members of the construction team had been meeting, sharing their discontent with each other and planning their course of action. It is fair to say that their perception of the difficulty was exacerbated by the pressure they were under. For 10 weeks, they had been working 10 hours a day, six days a week trying to remain on schedule.

The day before opening I spent in individual negotiations with every member of D&P. At the end of the day, I held a joint meeting. I wanted to be able to open with a team that was at least pasted back together enough to receive well-deserved congratulations. I found myself openly commiserating with some of the charges, but reiterating my support and loyalty to the supervisor who had worked devotedly and long for the museum. This meant letting people understand that I had made a decision and if they forced me to choose between them or him, I would choose him. I, and others, attempted to get everyone to soften their positions so that there would be no need for an immediate mass exodus.

We succeeded only partly. Some temporary members were scheduled to leave immediately anyway. We urged one uncompromising ringleader to leave, too. Some valued members' feelings never healed; these people left within the first six months. One outspoken member stuck it out and made her truce permanently with the leader. After all that work, the opening was only bittersweet for the D&P crew.

At two in the morning on the day before the opening, filled with fatigue and elation, I walked around the completed Exhibit Center, showing it to Mike, and I burst into tears.

Private Openings

On June 24, 1979, we began opening the museum with nine separate events. The smartest thing we did was to focus on ourselves first. Our first opening was exclusively for all the workers, including staff, volunteers and construction workers, and their immediate families. There was evident pride in being able to show all this work to one's children. This would reap benefits during the next weeks and long after.

We held an additional family event so that all TCM workers could invite any five members of their family, however they chose to define family. It was poignant to see parents of adult children congratulating each other for bringing these gifted people into the world. It was important to remember that we, as staff, needed to be recognized by our families, including our parents, even though we were "grown up."

A separate opening was held for professionals. All staff were allowed to define that term and invite colleagues as they saw fit. This allowed staff to thank the people who had helped them individually. Not only the board, directors and fund-raisers had "chits" outstanding; every single member of staff had asked for important favors within his or her own specialty and needed to repay them.

That evening, I gave a toast that saluted TCM staff and their monumental accomplishment. As I asked them to stand, an emotional roar went up from the crowd. Our staff were being cheered by their professional peers who understood best the meaning of their achievement.

Public Opening

We closed Jamaica Plain the day after April vacation week, a high attendance time, and remained closed during the traditionally slow months of May and June. We opened at the

Wharf on July 1, the beginning of the tourist season and the busiest two months in the calendar year. This meant that we could not practice operating with just a few people in the building, or orient ourselves before the crowds came. In the first 12 weeks, with the attendant promotion, 180,000 visitors came, the same number we served during the entire previous year.

The new exhibition environment was significantly different from the one we were used to, so that our try-outs in Jamaica Plain were not entirely relevant. At the Wharf site, we had more visitors, a reduced staff/visitor ratio and a radically different lay-out. While we had field-tested all the concepts and even sections of the exhibits, rarely had an exhibit been tested in its entirety.

The visitors came and touched our pristine interactive museum. Immediately, everything that could break, broke, and every system that could fail, failed. We wanted to rush on to the public space and yell "Go home! Stop messing it up!"

The staff primarily responsible for running the Jamaica Plain site while the rest of us installed, closed and packed it up now moved to the Wharf. They set up their office, hired and trained new staff and got ready to run the new museum. They had been left out of the excitement for a long time and felt quite heroic. Now they became the front line.

Every evening at closing, the operating managers got together and invented new systems to replace the ones that failed that day. Fortunately, we had a team of experienced staff whom we enfranchised to "punt" by inventing new systems on the spot. We promised we would reward, not punish, staff for individual initiative.

An example of a complex system that kept failing was the operation of the entrance hall with its ticketing function. When we planned the lobby we understood all the functions, worked with architects, had experienced staff ready, trained new staff and had many rehearsals. Even so, we knew we had a compromise situation because we had too many functions jammed into one place. Some of the elements we could contended with were the size, shape and location of the space, the speed of ticketing, the reliability of the computer, the need to get statistics, the traffic flow, signage, group orientation, the varying number of staff needed to match the hourly attendance curve, and handicap access. In some instances, the solution to one problem competed with and hindered solving another, no less important function. For example, faster ticketing moved the waiting line quickly, yet the best place to gather statistics was at the ticket desk, which then slowed down this process. We "took our best shot" at the operation of the lobby and only partially succeeded.

Things broke and systems did not work, but it was not because we hadn't anticipated the problems, or properly planned or trained. Rather, it was because we had not known how to solve some dilemmas. Therefore, we did not know how to repair them either. We remained optimistic for the first week or so when we thought we could correct the difficulties easily. In the next six months, we were depressed, though no less dogged, when it became apparent that the solutions were cumulative and minutely detailed. We would only fully understand the necessary steps retrospectively when whatever had been broken was finally fixed. In a process of closer and closer approximation, when each of the adjustments seemed insignificant, and when changing one element could create an entirely new situation, there was very little measurable satisfaction. The process was draining, and the pressure to get it right quickly was high. The staff needed constant optimistic support. It was an unglamorous time and followed immediately on the most enervating time of all, the rush to open. We tried to compensate by extolling publicly the "unsung heros" who were turning us into a fully functioning museum, but it seemed hollow as we slogged ahead.

We discovered, much to our surprise, that in order to fix any operation problem, we had to "throw money at it," often by hiring more staff. We also discovered we had to make the system more complex before we could simplify it again. Once the problem was solved, though we were now overstaffed, we could extrapolate and design a more efficient system for less people.

Although needing to revamp the staffing pattern, the operations staff felt guilty about spending unplanned money and so were caught in a bind. They didn't know if, by solving one problem, they were creating a new one—an unmanageable budget. They tried to do without, didn't ask for help soon enough and felt angry and defeated. When the problem was finally articulated, a decision was made by the directors and board to overspend the first year's budget. That at least allowed us to ease the strain.

A new problem arose. It was difficult to know what kind of commitment to make to new staff when hiring, because we did not know what would become of the new positions. Ultimately, in some instances, people and jobs remained. In other instances, jobs were abolished but the people stayed. In still other cases, jobs and people both went. At the time, we did not have clear job categories or any absolute differentiation among temporary, permanent and contract staff, although we used all those terms. We did not have clear compensation categories or criteria for job descriptions. Each division hired separately. It appeared that some people might be getting more money for the same work by working for one division over another or by being declared on contract rather than salary. This made the existing staff feel insecure as evident reorganization was going on. They were angry about perceived inequities. Had we predicted this need for hiring new, possibly temporary help, we could have allayed many of the staff fears.

Rest

At the time of the opening, we put a six-week moratorium on all vacations, thinking that we should have extra help immediately available to cover any unexpected emergency. As it turned out, we could use only trained floor staff and thus, we did not deploy the rest of the people we had held up.

Emotionally, everyone thought in two phases: before and after the opening. With the pressure of running the new museum, unpacking and beginning new courses, every member of the staff suddenly understood that the opening was not the end of anything but part of a continuum of seamless pressures. Everyone was physically exhausted and needed time off as a psychological pause between the move and the continuous operation of the institution. In retrospect, delaying vacations was a serious mistake.

Unpacking

The development people had been on site for two years, working in a trailer and assorted nearby offices. They wondered what the rest of us interlopers were doing there now. The operations people had moved weeks before the opening and had already partially unpacked. After the opening, the people most closely involved with the installation began to unpack.

The staff of the Resource Center—the division responsible for housing all the resource materials and for running outreach and multi-session programs—felt great strain. They wanted the public to see the variety of things they had to offer from the beginning. Since content specialists (developers) worked for both the Resource and the Exhibit Center and they had concentrated on installing their exhibits prior to opening, they had to focus on getting their resources and teaching materials unpacked immediately afterward.

Because every department had apportioned insufficient time to unpack, some staff took more than a year to get fully settled in. They always felt behind and rushed to catch up. This added to their feelings of disorientation and inefficiency, and led to their anger at management for being insensitive to their work needs.

Meeting on the Stairs

There were daily work schemes that all the staff had unconsciously integrated in Jamaica Plain. These had to do with meeting people on the stairs, in the bathrooms, by the mail boxes and on the way to and from meeting rooms. Staff members knew whom they sat next to and whom they would encounter as they progressed through their work day. People saved information for those seemingly random meetings and accomplished a great deal of sharing in that way. In moving to the Wharf, all these fragile and unconscious connections were broken. Staff could not automatically find the people they needed without a new, conscious plan. Similarly, equipment like copying machines appeared in unfamiliar locations and caused new and unfamiliar patterns of behavior to form.

Some people who previously were in the hub of things now found themselves isolated, and others who had gotten used to quiet now found their quarters noisy. Many of the same groups of people were housed together, but some new combinations had been made that required new staff connections. Some people missed their former office mates, while other staff found it exciting to be with new colleagues.

Watershed

Designers, fabricators, curators and developers had been in the limelight for many months before the opening and initial congratulations focused on them. Afterward, the operations people were the ascendant group and the others did not get much attention from management again for many months. It was difficult for some to take a back seat or, worse still, be caught up in the unglamorous work of repair. For some, preparing for the move had provided an opportunity to grow in their work, which now suddenly seemed truncated. Very few staff had left during the previous three years, so there had been no natural attrition. Everyone had wanted to stay in order to complete their piece of work, and be part of the family at opening. Now, for some, it was time to go.

Just a few weeks after opening, one of the three designers began looking for a new job. Three other long-term employees in senior management positions decided to leave at the same time. Each one felt a mixture of guilt and excitement, each had gained new skills and each wanted to move on to new independence and greater success. In addition, there was the expected leaving of the temporary crew of assistants and installers, as well as the two members of design and production who were involved in the previous hostilities with their supervisor. A single going-away party filled with skits, gags and serious gifts was held for the four senior people so that we would not have to exacerbate the painful good-byes.

Some of the rest of the staff began to feel that to remain was unadventurous and cowardly. The management, wanting to be supportive of everyone, set up a system of career counseling called "Watershed." All senior employees were given time with their supervisors to explore their futures. The question was, if they wanted to stay, How could we redraft a job description that would allow for new growth? Or, if they wanted to go, How could we help them with career planning and recommendations, as a sign of our gratitude? Many people misunderstood the managers' intentions and decided that Watershed was a code word for ousting staff, cleverly disguised in the form of help. Management unwittingly had added to the problem.

Soon, however, whoever wanted to leave did so, and a new commitment was made by those who wished to continue.

Nostalgia, No Previous History

During the entire first year, the only common daily recollections the staff shared concerned our previous location, which led to eulogizing Jamaica Plain. Only later, after we had spent a year at the Wharf, did this diminish.

Many staff believed that at the Wharf we had lost our sense of family, that things were too big and too bureaucratic. We had become, indeed, more bureaucratized in an attempt to get disrupted systems to work and in order to run a larger and more complex organization. Our full-time staff grew from 70 to 85. An important part of the change was the expansion of the middle management level. It came about rather informally and gave supervisory responsibilities to people who were not prepared for them. We created departments where there used to be individuals, often making the individual the "head" without much warning or training. These people felt unsupported as they learned and guilty if mistakes were made. Some of the new "managers" left soon afterward because they did not feel suited for the new jobs.

A significant number of staff were newcomers. The staff divided into two groups: those who had worked in the previous site, and those who had not. There was social cache in being in the old-timers crowd, and phrases like "new team" and "old team" sprang up to differentiate staffs. New staff often felt left out when old staff talked about the old site with affection. The new staff felt that they had missed the golden age.

"Things are not as good as they once were" and "In the good old days in JP . . . " colored many of our sentences. We needed to remind ourselves that JP had been full of blemishes and was not golden all the time. We needed to remember that we moved because we had to. Nevertheless, it was difficult to temper the nostalgia with more realism. People despaired that while the move was very successful for the public, life would never be as good again for the staff.

Our style in Jamaica Plain had been very informal. We had dressed casually. In moving to the Wharf, many of us had come to believe that we had to dress differently and have better "manners." While we tried to combat the prevailing notion that "company was coming" and that we should be on our best behavior, we did not altogether succeed. Our publicity brought many "famous" people to our door. Our exhibition style and our public spaces were indeed more glamorous than they had been and some believed we had to "grow up" to match them. Others believed we had become too slick, had gotten our priorities wrong and were being seduced by the "big time."

Mike and the Re-establishment of the Mission

The three division directors realized there was a widespread feeling that we had lost our way and were in danger of becoming a different kind of institution. We asked Mike to clear his calendar of all appointments and to walk around the museum, to reassert his tone and his view of the institution in a casual but continuous way. Six weeks after opening, every day for a month, Mike, wearing informal clothes, did just that. He saw all the staff in his travels, heard all the complaints and saw to small improvements in the building. Had Mike been changed by the move, or had he forgotten our goals and mission, this strategy might have exacerbated the problem. By his calm, unadorned and consistent manner, he reassured us that our confusion was temporary.

Staff Unrest

Six months after opening, although we had made many improvements to the operational systems, staff did not feel that the new museum was attending to their needs. They started to hold ad hoc meetings, intentionally excluding directors, in order to consolidate their grievances. The meetings were highly charged and attendance was determined by position in the hierarchy. Meetings were held that invited section heads; other meetings excluded them and section heads held their own meetings.

When prepared, the staff called a meeting with the directors to present their demands. They saw themselves as loyal and devoted staff who had been taken for granted and abused. There was considerable heat and anger.

Their demands were of two basic kinds:

First they wanted a personnel committee formed to which they had access and membership. They wanted the compensation system overhauled so that job categories would be created and job descriptions written that would ensure more equitable pay for equivalent work.

Second, they wanted a centrally located staff lounge.

Staff could be seen talking animatedly everywhere and conversation would often stop when a manager entered a room. Feelings ran high. Staff worried that their demands would be ignored or that retaliation would ensue for staff leaders. Instead, Mike took the position that the proposals were important and in the best interest of the entire museum. The demands were immediately acted upon and changed the priorities of the directors' work.

The Lounge and the Personnel Committee

The Personnel Committee, with elected representatives, was formed and met monthly with all the directors. Many of the representatives were the originators of the discontent. Within the first year, the committee, together with the management group, produced a new personnel handbook that included job categories, compensation levels, rules for hiring and discipline.

We opened a staff lounge almost immediately. This lounge was never very successful and remained a continuous issue. We learned that it was not enough to allocate space, equipment or money to form a successful meeting space. Subtle ingredients were at play, such as where it was located, whether it was seen to be "owned" by one group of staff to the exclusion of another or whether food could be prepared there. However, at the time of the agitation, the management group felt that all demands were urgent and should be seen to immediately. A less than adequate lounge seemed better than no lounge at all. This was not a matter of cynicism. The management group believed that if the staff felt so assertive, they must also be right. Surprisingly, acceding to demands was not seen as weakness. It was felt that if staff and management were to become a partnership, then those matters formerly overlooked by management should be corrected by them.

The staff was skeptical but impressed that their demands were taken seriously. The matter of forging new personnel policy brought workers into continuous contact with management and allowed all involved to experience the process of joint decision making. The work of this committee went a long way toward re-establishing the museum's "culture" of open consensus-building.

My Depression

This staff agitation, while thoughtful and constructive, caused me to become personally depressed. I had worked for five years toward the move. I felt successful in accomplishing the installation and was proceeding in the effort of debugging the operations scheme. While different staff groups were under extreme stress during different stages of the move, as their supervisor, I had not let up. I was worn out, needed "mercy" and tending, and was not up to taking on another issue. While I understood that my role was to serve as the lightning rod for staff frustration and that I was not to confuse it with my personal life, there came a time when I could not do that successfully. I felt guilty and threatened by their allegations, and became defeated, lethargic and relatively unresponsive. During the next six months, I limped along doing my job only adequately until I slowly healed and returned to the optimism and enthusiasm that the job demanded.

End of the Long-Range Plan

One year later, at a conference that Mike attended, participants were asked to raise their hands if their institution had a formal long-range plan in effect. Mike raised his hand proudly and then slowly lowered it, for he realized that we had used up our plan within the first year.

During that time, we learned to run the building, re-established our internal sense of community, became more informal again (though we would never be quite as unstructured) and began to dream new dreams. We also sustained two staff deaths, four divorces, three marriages and the birth of two new babies.

On the anniversary of our first year, we awarded each other "survivor" T-shirts. The picture on the front—our logo bunny valiantly treading water in our logo gumball machine—suggested that while we often felt like we were drowning, we had come through and would go on.

Reflections and Recommendations

The literature on institutional change suggests that change is divided into two distinct categories: voluntary and involuntary. Voluntary change is preferable because it can be planned for, while involuntary change, such as natural disasters, can only be reacted to. Moving the museum would be classified as a voluntary decision and it was certainly planned for. But in truth, it was only voluntary for the senior staff and the board who made the initial decision. For the staff, the choice ultimately was either to move with us or leave. Similarly, for some of the staff, the planning felt reactive rather than proactive.

The move colored our work lives for years and permanently affected our relationships with each other and our audience. Sometimes we felt like a family uprooted because a parent had been transferred to a new and better job. All other family members understood that they were neither the valued kin nor the deciding factor, yet they had to move, leaving the familiar behind. During the transition, it would be fair to categorize each of us as taking on, in succession, all the various family roles from the dependent, often recalcitrant child to the adventurous parent.

In retrospect, we planned and collectively did many things correctly. These either averted or reduced potential difficulties. We tend to remember the gaffes most vividly, but it is useful to review the good, because our tendency to underrate our successes would present the reader with an uneven picture. I find I want to be quite "Pollyanna-ish" about it all, because the lessons that were so hard won at the time seem self-evident only in retrospect.

Participatory Decision Making and Tone

We encouraged and rewarded independent decision making in all areas. Where staff had real expertise, they were encouraged to discover and try out systems without necessarily checking with supervisors. There was genuine respect among staff and many supported each other in ways that transcended their job descriptions. The worry that independence might lead to anarchy was unfounded, and although eventually we formalized some rules, what was known in the museum as "guerilla action" or "punting" is still a rewarded part of our culture.

We encouraged bonding, ceremonies and rituals from the outset. These events were genuine expressions of the spirit and playfulness of the museum and not artificially imposed. They added pleasure to the stressful time, added to the mythology that was retold later and were a waste of neither time nor money. Rituals continue to be supported and expanded.

At the opening events, we understood the important adage "Always thank everyone," but we received unexpected rewards by trumpeting ourselves first. In the rush to acknowledge donors and trustees, staff are often forgotten or desultorily mentioned. If not appropriately recognized, staff can carry resentment forever, and they will remind you of your failing later when the going gets tough. There is always the danger that staff will receive the congratulations as pro forma, gratuitous or insincere. But staff not only deserve our appreciation, it is an important ingredient toward building staff morale.

Planning

The openness of the decision making process was the most supportive element for staff. They were included formally in planning from the beginning. Everything was revealed and all levels of hierarchy were able to contribute. I learned that sharing information was not as dangerous as I had been led to believe and making it available was a helpful, not destructive, activity. This access allowed staff to trust that decisions were not arbitrary and that their concerns would be heard and respected, if not always agreed to. The manager had to be prepared for anger when conflicting opinions inevitably made winners and losers of some staff, or if anyone was overruled. But I believe there was less anger than if the decisions had seemed capricious or uninformed.

Initially some of us wondered what relevance we had to the planning process and were skeptical about participating. Our horizon line was relatively short and the press of our work very great. We thought long-range planning was the director's job, not ours. Focusing on long-term issues struck many of us as irrelevant, or interference in the daily routine. In order to get willing compliance, management must recognize how much time planning takes. Management should not expect staff to graft meetings onto their daily work.

Because both board and staff served on the same planning committee, each side benefited by getting to know the other better and appreciating each other's concerns. Thereafter, board members would talk knowledgeably about program issues, when in other arenas. Staff likewise had a new perspective that had been outside their own purview. The potential danger of the board and staff members bypassing the director by dealing directly with each other outside of this forum did not happen in our case, as each side was respectful of the rules.

We continued to have all levels of staff participate in planning, with ongoing benefits. Staff are members of the Personnel Committee, Health and Safety Committee and the Long-Range Policy Committee. Staff elections to the Personnel Committee have continued and the committee has allowed the staff to bring their priorities to a forum for change, review and amendment. The elected members become knowledgeable about the particular issues. They absorb the process of running groups, watch managers function first hand and understand holistically the difficulty of making a complex decision. Ultimately, they serve as conduits of information to and from the rest of the staff.

Resistance to Change

For many of us, the move involved learning new skills and information. For example, I had to learn to work with architects, curators had to examine climate control systems and designers needed to research new materials. Some of us felt exposed because we believed we should have known this information already. We became fearful that we would be found out, and we were tempted to hide our ignorance. On reflection, it is logical that part of the staff's expected resistance to change comes from their anxiety about new information. The next time around, I would acknowledge to the staff (and myself) that learning is both exciting and anxiety-provoking. I would recognize, and make allowance for, the time it takes to acquire new information. While we provided formal training in some cases, we were not systematic enough about identifying our areas of inexperience, and much learning was done unevenly and under pressure.

Group Behavior

Throughout the move I had to distinguish among the individual, the small group and the entire institution. Each was a separate entity with its own culture and its own need. I had to learn to treat each group in terms of itself.

A group, I discovered, would tolerate some behavioral deviation from individuals it admired and would chastise or otherwise discipline those members it did not tolerate. Our institution valued some amount of eccentric behavior, and the staff made allowances—although not without some grumbling—for the creative "genius" who needed someone to clean up after him. A group whose culture was full of games accepted members who did not want to play; they could safely be watchers rather than joiners. However, if they overtly shunned the group, they would be excluded. When discipline was done within the norms of the group and within the institutional tone, I learned not to interfere. However, sometimes scapegoating happened that was very destructive and needed to be stopped.

Within the group, the jokes could be so private and the culture so seemingly exclusive that a divided society of "them and us" would form. I was torn between the enjoyment of the group's cohesiveness and the alienation the rest of us felt. Realistically, I could have only a marginal effect on this problem anyway.

While working on the installation, first with the design and production staff and then with the curators, I discovered that each staff member simultaneously belonged to a collective whole and to specialized subsets delineated by task. The subgroup often faced stress in relative isolation. The members believed that neither I, as their supervisor, nor the rest of the workers as a whole, understood or appreciated their predicament. They felt abandoned and angry. The group needed to be reassured that their concerns were real and relevant. I needed to be honest and disclose my position on every issue so they knew what I would and would not advocate. They needed to be reminded of the competing forces and the limits of my power.

The Trials of Being a Manager

When staff needed me to fix a situation that was holding up their work, they often had unrealistic expectations about what I could accomplish. Depending on the outcome, they thought either that I had unlimited power or that I was powerless. Contrary to my previous training, I learned that if I explained the cause of the limits of my power, I was not necessarily revealing weakness. Instead, I was introducing a note of realism and was asking staff to include me on their side. "We are all in this together."

However, as a manager I often had to say, "I have decided. . . . That's settled! We move on!" Many decisions were part of complex, unfolding situations rather than discreet events. Because the process was shared with the staff on an ongoing basis, they could watch managers re-examine decisions in order to weigh the pros and cons and sometimes change their minds. This led staff to believe that managers were indecisive and/or unsure. Sometimes they were right. Occasionally, as managers, we had a bout of nerves or truly did not know what to do. Sometimes, unknown to staff, new information had come in.

Thus we appeared arbitrary if we closed issues that staff continued to advocate and indecisive if issues remained open when the staff wanted us to take a position—any position. Staff felt that they could not always count on previously announced agreements, and that all solid ground might shift. These judgments by staff of the managers' performance were not unique to the move, but mirrored other management situations.

There were moments when I announced that I would no longer serve as a punching bag and that I had had enough: "I am a person too!" During the stress of the move, I learned that I as a manager and I as a person did not have to be inexorably separated. Remarkably, the staff learned to differentiate needing me as manager from supporting me as an individual.

Finally I accepted my own limits in effecting change in the staff's attitudes. Despite what I had been taught previously, people did not so much work for as with me. Being "boss" was a job, like being a carpenter. It only commanded the respect and power that I earned and others wanted to give.

Dislocation

The specter of moving engendered unrealistic optimism: people visualized spaces that were better than possible. Some staff believed that because they had attended meetings about the proposed office space, they had been promised whatever they had asked for. There was an inevitable let-down when they came face to face with reality and had to give up their fantasies. When it became clear that the new reality was truly worse than the previous location (as it was in some cases), then anger seemed an appropriate consequence. From my vantage point, the staff was very tolerant and good-humored about living in unfinished space for six subsequent years. I came to believe that there must be subtle ingredients, in addition to beauty and seeming comfort, that make for supportive office space. We must have had some but by no means all of them in our makeshift back rooms to sustain so much camaraderie.

Staff personalized their offices with a collage of treasures that became the design norm. They overcame the lack of privacy by working at home, or sometimes by commandeering closets and turning them into meeting rooms. It became clear that one essential ingredient for the staff's well-being was having a sound-proof private area where they could speak freely to each other or to a manager without embarrassment and without being watched over.

Placement of staff within offices caused friendships and partnerships to evolve. Continuous offices allowed colleagues to discover joint work just by walking by and casually chatting. It is important, therefore, when contemplating a move to understand that the proximity of staff to each other will help shape the future program of the institution.

Placement should be designated with great care.

I discovered that I did not walk through the institution on my way to my office if I did not have to. Nor did the rest of the staff. The museum can become an abstract place if it is easily bypassed by an elevator or the back stairs. Our connectedness to the institution was improved by placing our offices within the exhibition spaces. Our tempers were not.

In the beginning, we did not realize how important the placement of informal congre-gating areas—such as the switchboard, the mailboxes, the vending machines, the lounge and lunch place, the staff bathrooms and the sign-in and sign-out locations—were to the emotional climate. They were the most heterogeneous locations, cutting across division lines and hierarchies, and were used by all staff to see each other, exchange pleasantries and information. Once we understood this, we took great care in relocating these areas. We had to learn that confusion and disorientation were part of the settling-in process. We should have compensated for the loss of sharing by, for example, adding more frequent staff meetings and publishing in-house newsletters more often.

The most basic lesson we learned when we moved staff and equipment was that work was slowed down until new patterns were formed. In the beginning, we should have allowed extra time for finishing tasks and acknowledged staff frustration when they accomplished less.

We thought, inaccurately, that once the museum was reopened, staff numbers would go down. We found we needed extra staff for operations and for unpacking. I would rec-ommend planning for some unexpected over-staffing in the beginning and hold a discre-tionary reserve account to be used to solve difficult problems. Streamlining was a good goal but it only became a reality six months later.

Recovery

We were exhausted by the time we opened. We never gave ourselves permission to rest or recover. In retrospect, I would advise giving vacations to all staff first, then allowing ample time for unpacking and setting up before beginning any new courses or work-shops. It was not fair to ask staff to both unpack and begin new work simultaneously. Our tendency was to pretend that unpacking was a casual chore that could be fitted in.

If opening occurs during a busy season, I would go so far as to suggest that mandatory vacations be instituted as close to the opening as possible. Alternatively, and better still, one should open at a quiet time, shakedown in peace and give staggered though leisurely vacations before the active season comes upon you. System failure is often embarrassing and staff is better protected if shakedown is done in relative privacy.

The actual move and installation were adrenalin-packed events. There was an inevitable let-down afterward. The director needs to understand that the staff might feel that the institution has lost its way and needs to re-establish its tone and vision. The director should be prepared to disregard new work in order to encounter all staff often and in the most casual way. This is no time to be remote or austere.

As unexpected as it was for me, it now seems perfectly logical that staff unrest occurred and focused on personnel issues, especially compensation, benefits and compensatory time. The speed of change in the new museum forced managers to make up some personnel policies as they went along. This resulted in unevenness. The staff needed clarity and uniformity that we could have provided only by thinking through the new personnel issues in advance. Even though we had revised the personnel policy before we moved, it did not accurately forecast the new situation. With the pressure of the opening period, we would not have thought to work on the personnel policy immediately after opening had the staff not demanded it. An expanded personnel policy manual that is appropriate to the new situation should be made a serious part of the moving plans.

Summary

Moving is such a huge dislocation that even if you manage to do everything right, you and your staff will still have to endure a long and difficult recovery period. Some things have to be lived through; they cannot be bypassed. Therefore it is not a reasonable goal for any manager to strive for a "traumaless" trauma.

Emotional regrouping takes at least a year. It makes sense to consolidate and rest. It is very important to enjoy your collective accomplishment and to glory in it. Yet in the midst of the turmoil, if you, as managers, have not begun to dream new dreams and to formulate new plans, you will not be ready to take your institution forward when it is again time to take on new challenges.

I believe that no matter what you do:

During the process of moving, the whole staff will go through a predictable cycle of feelings and actions. These will be:

In the beginning: excitement, unrealistic optimism, disbelief, skepticism, detachment

During the installation: helpfulness, creativity, hard work, humor, fatigue, frustration and anger

After the opening: pride, diligence, nostalgia, lethargy, disillusionment, depression, anger and agitation

People will leave, people will stay, new staff will come, the spirit will have to be rebuilt.

You can make things worse by not paying attention, by patronizing or by being punitive. Remember, all of you have moved.

To make it better you should, as manager:

Acknowledge that mood swings are to be expected and that they affect work.

Understand that dislocation is disorienting and make allowances for it.

Make new rituals and preserve some old ones, but make sure that as much humanization and personalization as possible is introduced into the new space.

Be generous with rest and vacations.

Take care of yourself. There is a limit to what you can tolerate. Announce this fact.

Acknowledge miscalculations and go about correcting them. Having to live with errors without redress furthers frustration.

Encourage peer support.

Make communication safe. It is more likely that you will be in the information loop and can take action early if you are told what is going on.

Allow as much information as possible to be available so that "above ground" is more powerful than the underground.

Separate issues from emotion, but take both seriously. The problems the staff focus on have probably been festering unattended for a long time and need to be solved positively. The feelings may be inevitable, but they are powerful and threatening for the staff. They need emotional support.

Establish tone and boundaries. Emotional anarchy is also disruptive. Work needs to go on and is itself a great healer.

Wander about, be seen and be available.

Delay new work and live off the newness of the move for as long as possible. At the same time, begin new dreams as realistically as possible so that new goals can produce measurable accomplishments and new sources of pride.

Now

I have not spoken enough about our pride in our work. We were proud then and continue to think that what we accomplished was worthwhile.

Many of the staff members who moved are still at the museum 16 years later. Within a few years after the move, staff hardly spoke of Jamaica Plain anymore. They felt as though they had always been at the Wharf, or at least for a long, indeterminate time.

In the intervening years, more staff left. In 1986, after 23 years at the museum, Michael Spock left to spearhead the reconceptualization, redesign and installation of large portions of the exhibitions at the Field Museum in Chicago. In 1987, 16 years after I had started at The Children's Museum, I left as well and moved to Washington, D.C., to participate in starting, changing, building or opening five different museums and museum-like projects. I, who had believed that we have stamina for only one such trauma in our professional lives, went on to make a career of it.

Between 1979 and 1995, the Children's Museum has had two additional directors and suffered through a recession that was particularly severe on the East Coast. Yet through those changes and the concomitant pain, the museum and the staff within it never faltered in their commitment to each other and to the vision they had forged so long ago. The museum's staff and mission have sometimes seemed a little battered, but they have endured. To their credit, the staff of the Boston Children's Museum remains full of dreams and continues to do excellent work.

I have worked for three different and wonderful organizations during this 16-year period. While each had its own interesting ethos, I never again found the special community spirit that seemed so ordinary when I was in Boston.

Mitigating Staff Stress in a Natural Disaster

The Charleston Museum, Charleston, S.C.

John R. Brumgardt

The wisdom of emergency planning among museums in recent years has been emphasized by natural disasters such as floods, earthquakes and hurricanes. These plans, appropriately, focus on securing cultural and physical resources. However, personnel should likewise be considered, for their well-being is critical to an organization's ability to protect its resources and remain viable despite the impact of a disaster.

The Charleston Museum's experience with Hurricane Hugo in 1989 demonstrated the immediate and long-term importance of providing as stable an environment as possible for staff both before and after a crisis. This is essential if the organization is to perform effectively and convert a disaster to a reference point for future strength and confidence.

Located immediately on the coast of South Carolina, Charleston historically has been subject to hurricanes. Their periodic destruction through the centuries has generated a continuing consciousness of vulnerability that is emphasized by area geography. Known as the "Lowcountry," much of the region is but a few feet above sea level, unprotected from the incoming power of ocean storms.

"Hurricane season" begins in June and extends through October. Anxious times can arise throughout, but September is traditionally the month of most concern. Prior to 1989, no serious storm had occurred for several years. Longtime residents, though, insisted that we were "due for a big one." Our museum made plans to accommodate it. And at around midnight on September 21, Hurricane Hugo—a massive storm—came ashore. This chapter recounts the impact of that disaster, how we attempted to mitigate its effect on staff, and the positive outcome that resulted.

Background/Advance Planning

Founded in 1773, The Charleston Museum preserves the social and natural history of the South Carolina coastal region. Collections and research focus on history, archaeology, ornithology, documentary materials and natural science. Facilities include the main museum building, three historic houses (two of them National Historic Landmarks) and a wildlife sanctuary containing multiple archaeological sites and earthen Civil War batteries. The museum and houses are located in the downtown peninsula, while the sanctuary is situated on nearby James Island. A nonprofit organization, the museum depends substantially on earned income, and visitation fees comprise more than 40 percent of all annual revenues. This, then, is a multi-site operation, with limited staff, whose funding is heavily reliant on tourism. These factors are significant in our capacity to sustain the impact of a major natural disaster.

Among many initial priorities following my arrival as director in March 1984 was creating the organization's first written emergency plan. As was true with other planning efforts, this process involved the active participation of all principal staff and review/approval by the board of trustees. The result was therefore a product of consensus. Since the plan was developed in the absence of direct practical experience, we knew that it could not anticipate all contingencies. Still, it was carefully and deliberately devised, and everyone had stock in its effective implementation. The plan was completed none too soon, for a hurricane approached the coast in September 1984 and emergency preparations were first put into effect.

Fortunately, as occurred with periodic threats during the next five years, the storm went elsewhere and our efforts amounted to practice drills. Although stressful and time-consuming, these experiences were invaluable. Implemented under real storm-threat conditions, they provided a practical training ground where assumptions and expectations were tested and familiarity with one another, under genuine pressure, developed. Performance critiques following each situation helped us to remedy deficiencies in our planning, to identify and accommodate previously unrecognized contingencies and to more fully understand our collective and individual capabilities.

The Human Factor

Tensions grow incrementally—usually for several days—as a storm makes its way across the ocean. Earthquakes and tornadoes, for example, occur unexpectedly, but hurricanes provide a worrisome, unreliable warning that nourishes apprehensions. Unpredictable in speed, course and velocity, they can be taunting, frustrating and frightening. Weather service prognostications grow in frequency as storms approach the Caribbean Sea and East Coast, but these are only best-guess indicators concerning ultimate landfall. News media, meanwhile, alert citizens to the possibility of terrible destruction. The general atmosphere becomes one of nervous speculation.

During such periods, staff face the mixed challenge of considering how to fulfill their job responsibilities while also caring for their homes, families and possibly unique personal circumstances. Persons requiring regular medication, working-parent families and those with disabled or elderly dependents, for instance, are particularly affected, while staff members living in beach areas are more vulnerable than those whose homes are inland. Besides these variable, competing concerns, staff are also susceptible, like everyone else, to prevailing anxieties. They may therefore experience real conflicts when confronting an emergency.

Storm preparations before 1989 made us acutely aware of these factors. "Trial runs" demonstrated that advance readiness, on an established alert basis, was essential to effective preparations and to minimizing both individual and collective staff apprehensions. Our emergency plan had originally called for implementation to begin only when ordered by the director, regardless of the status of a storm. However, it became apparent that remanding action to one individual's subjective judgment only compounded the uncertainty of the situation, exacerbated tensions and accommodated neither the exigencies of pre-storm conditions nor the dispersed living locations of staff members in an area characterized by waterways and bridges. If the call came during non-working hours, for example, blinding rains or flooding might make it impossible for many to return to the museum.

We revised our plans in view of these practical lessons in an effort to improve performance and create maximum predictability in the face of anxious circumstances. We determined that the emergency plan would be activated on a scheduled basis (when a "watch" was declared), not in a last-minute rush. Also, anticipating situations where a storm threat might become imminent at night or on a weekend, we decided to activate plans in advance when necessary, while staff were on the job. In short, we attempted to accommodate the various contingencies that experience had taught us to expect.

The Logistics of Preparation

Preparing for a storm is a large and expensive undertaking for us. Emergency supplies, for example, must be replenished. In addition, because hurricanes occur during Charleston's busy summer/fall tourist season (one of our two principal income periods of the year), closing the museum and historic houses interrupts our essential cash flow. Moreover, we have a limited number of staff (42 full-time personnel in 1989) and physically separate facilities to prepare. Because other municipal and nonprofit agencies are engaged in their own preparations, all work must be accomplished by museum staff.

The historic houses contain extensive collections of furniture and decorative arts objects. Built in the late 18th and early 19th centuries, these are large, three-story masonry structures. Objects (identified in advance) must be packed, moved and stored; carpets must be rolled; shutters must be secured; and so forth. Curators who, with the house administrators, helped to draft protective measures for these collections, must assist houses personnel in addition to carrying out their responsibilities at the museum.

The bulk of our collections and exhibitions, and all administrative and financial records, are located in the museum building. This is a modern, two-story brick structure of approximately 68,400 square feet. It is framed in an essential square, centering on an interior courtyard, and features extensive glass window walls on three sides. The upper floor, safe from possible flooding, contains principal exhibitions, collections storage and archives. Essential records, backup computer files and electronic equipment from ground floor offices must be relocated here; furniture must be moved and covered with plastic; gift shop materials must be stored; exterior furniture must be secured; and the like. In sum, preparation alone is a physically taxing and emotionally stressful activity.

Before the Storm

The first three-quarters of 1989 were enviable for the museum in terms of visitation, revenue production and overall progress. Feelings of accomplishment, though, were offset by sadness at the death of our assistant director in May, followed by general staff indignation concerning an unusual legal challenge to the museum, which went on for months. By fall, we looked forward to finishing the year and beginning anew. All we had to do was get through the hurricane season.

No hurricane of unusual force had struck Charleston for decades, and we hoped that this season would again spare us. In early September, however, Hurricane Gabrielle signaled possible problems. This was a powerful storm, with wind speeds of 120 miles per hour. We were relieved when it turned north, far out at sea. But such feelings were short-lived. Within only a few days an even stronger new storm formed in the Atlantic and moved rapidly westward. The eighth hurricane of the season, it was named Hugo.

By noon on Saturday, September 16, Hugo was just east of the island of Guadeloupe, moving west/northwest with wind speeds of 150 mph. This was surely a storm to take seriously, and we watched its course closely. It was so distant, though, that no weekend staff recall was required. Everyone hoped that, like Gabrielle, Hugo would turn north. Instead, it maintained a westerly direction. Two days later its winds had diminished in strength to 125 mph and the storm was about 1,200 miles away, moving northwest at 10 mph. Its ultimate destination was uncertain, but hurricane advisories were issued for Florida, Georgia and South Carolina.

Our staff met to review the situation on Monday, September 18. Florida and Georgia appeared potentially to be most in danger, and the national hurricane center predicted only a 4 percent chance that Hugo would strike Charleston. The storm's strength and size were so unusual, however, that we placed everyone on alert, double-checked our staff recall list, and replenished our emergency supplies. In the meantime, we also dealt with routine work including board meetings, an irate tour operator seeking preferred schedules at our historic houses, finalizing the museum's new drug-free workplace policy, grant applications, preliminary annual budget planning and master planning for our new wildlife sanctuary. Amid this, we regularly monitored reports of the hurricane's progress.

By 9:00 a.m. the next day, September 19, Hugo was still almost 900 miles from Charleston. Nevertheless, its diameter was now larger than the state of South Carolina and it seemed inevitable that we would experience at least tropical storm conditions even if the center struck elsewhere. Accordingly, although no hurricane watch had been declared by the weather service, we decided to begin preparations. While reports still predicted contact in Florida or Georgia, we considered it prudent to ensure readiness. Other Charleston cultural agencies did the same.

Beginning early gave us time to prepare deliberately, and things in general went smoothly. This was fortunate, for by the next day, September 20, apprehensions intensified as local wisdom declared that Hugo was headed here. One board member, for example, at the close of a meeting that evening, said that he would see me next month "if there's anything left of Charleston." Maintaining current track of the storm was difficult because radio reports were often hours old, and it became impossible to contact the weather service directly. The news media warned citizens to evacuate, and public shelters were activated. Elected officials appeared on television that night, predicting a hurricane of a force unknown in living memory and urging citizens to get away while there was still time.

General tension was now accentuated by hurried public buying. Supplies become scarce as worried shoppers filled gasoline tanks and bought essentials such as plywood, canned goods, bread, bottled water, batteries, candles and lamp oil. Propane became dear, camp stoves were not to be found in local stores and anxieties prevailed. Local tour operators, nevertheless, continued to accommodate visitors, and one guide in particular was upset that our facilities were closed. She wanted to take a group to one of our historic houses the next day and demanded to know why we could not reopen the place for just an hour. There was, then, no proverbial calm before the storm.

As had been true with preparations in past years, most staff faithfully carried out their respective assignments but a few participated only partially. One, for example, panicked, failed to back up important computer records and left town for safety. Denial or disregard of the threat, overt fear and attention to personal concerns seemed to determine the nature and degree of nonparticipation. In such circumstances there is no time for counseling or discipline; others have to do the work left undone. The majority worked efficiently and deserve real credit. Our security guard, for example, remained with his wife in the museum building throughout the storm to monitor events and provide protection. Preparations continued on the 21st, and then staff were released to take care of their homes and families.

Hurricane Hugo

Viewing the blue skies and soft white clouds on Thursday morning, September 21, a newly arrived visitor might have wondered at the boarded-up buildings and lines of vehicles leaving the vicinity. Evacuation had been ordered in many local communities and was urged throughout the area. Hugo had regained strength. Now at 135 mph, it was a dangerous Category 4 hurricane. Moreover, its forward speed had increased. By 9:00 p.m.

Hugo was less than 150 miles from Charleston. High winds and storm clouds presaged its coming. Still, as if to emphasize the unpredictable nature of such storms and the weather information available to us, radio reports continued to name Savannah as the most likely point of landfall.

Hugo struck Charleston at midnight on September 21. With sustained winds of 135 mph, it was the most powerful storm to hit South Carolina in decades. Strangely, its actual arrival provided momentary relief from the tension of waiting. This, however, was supplanted by new and greater anxieties concerning its impact. As one local reporter wrote in retrospect a year later, "It came in darkness. . . . We were blindfolded. Handcuffed. Helpless. Left to gauge the degree of danger with only our imagination. And through the night we could only imagine the worst. And with the first light of dawn, we learned it was even worse than we imagined."

Because local television and radio stations lost power early in the storm, persons in other states by the next morning frequently knew more about Hugo's effects than those who had lived through it. In fact, it had maintained terrible force as it moved inland, ravaging much of the state and then turning toward North Carolina. No one knew its final results and speculation was fueled by rumors and spotty news reports. Some broadcasts erroneously declared that "Charleston is gone," and that the historic district and all major public buildings had been destroyed. With this in mind, it now was time to review the damage.

After the Storm

Anxieties concerning Hugo's impact were quickly superseded by astonishment at the results. Devastation in the city and in outlying communities was shocking: mature trees were twisted and snapped; flattened houses stood alongside some pierced by tree limbs and others practically untouched; roofs and windows were damaged or destroyed; beachfront homes were blown and washed away; debris of every kind filled streets and yards; and power lines lay useless.

Personal reactions included virtual disbelief: How could this be true? Then, a range of questions: What has happened to the museum . . . to our historic houses and wildlife sanctuary . . . to my community? How will I care for my family? How can we recover from this? Then, resentment. The hurricane left a sense of personal violation by an impersonal force; a leveling, indiscriminate destruction; an initial feeling of overwhelming burden.

It was a challenge in such circumstances to undertake objective assessment of damages at our facilities. Because local telephone lines remained in operation, our security guard was able to inform us that the museum, although damaged, was basically secure. Other sites required personal reconnaissance by assigned staff. While extensive, the problems fortunately proved to be principally structural and repairable.

Thanks to the initiative of our building superintendent and his assistant, who reached the museum soon after the storm to repair localized roof damage, penetration of rainwater into our storage area was prevented. Glass breakage was substantial but all broken windows were on the building's interior and looting was not a threat. A recently completed firearms exhibit had been damaged when an adjacent window wall blew out, but this was the only direct impact on collections at the museum. Roof and window damages at the historic houses had resulted in some rainwater intrusion, but the objects were soon cared for and the damages patched. The Dill Sanctuary was not so lucky—we lost hundreds of trees—but cleanup, although enormous in scope, could be accomplished and the land would heal in time.

While some basic services were restored shortly, many were unavailable for days after the hurricane. There was initially no electricity, no water for toilets, drinking or bathing, and no gasoline. Most banks and other businesses were closed. Local television and radio stations were off the air. Schools and day-care centers could not open. Getting from one place to another was often difficult. Fallen trees blocked roads, debris clogged drains and caused flooding. After-dark curfews were declared to deter robbery and looting. Tire-puncturing nails from damaged roofs littered streets. And rain continued to fall. As laborers from other states filled the city to "help rebuild Charleston," huge debris-laden trucks rumbled continually and the sound of chain saws filled the air for weeks.

This was the depressing setting in which recovery had to occur. Commendably, while tense and exhausted, most people were soon determined to "put things back the way they were." At the museum, we felt the same way.

Recovery

One of our first priorities was to identify the situation of each staff member. This may seem routine. However, it is a major effort when faced with myriad storm-related problems. Some had lost their homes or experienced devastating damage; others suffered moderate loss. Regardless, all were significantly affected. Even if one's house was habitable, neighbors needed assistance in removing fallen trees, patching damaged roofs, obtaining water, cooking food and so forth. The storm had impact on virtually the entire state, and no relief appeared for days.

This was a time of anguish and uncertainty. Both landscape and life had changed, and the future in many respects appeared questionable. It would, indeed, have been easy to take emotional refuge in a general despair, but despair does not rebuild. Prevailing circumstances made it difficult to emphasize the future. But that is what we did at The

Charleston Museum. It was clearly necessary, to ensure recovery and organizational vitality, that we maintain a sense of stability and direction, reassure staff that this part of their lives would remain constant, and demonstrate that the museum would support its people.

Layoffs and joblessness became common following Hugo. Indeed, some business owners had urged employees to file for unemployment compensation even before the storm. Naturally, rumors flew and staff wondered what would occur. Our income flow had basically ceased. Recovery expenses would be substantial, and tourism had come to an essential halt. Where would the money come from?

Our board of trustees provided the answer by generously committing cash reserves to keep everyone employed and to finance recovery costs. Local governments, meanwhile, continued to provide regularly budgeted monthly allotments. Thanks to this support, all staff members were assured that their jobs were secure and that their paychecks would come regularly. Those who could not report because of serious damage were paid as if they had been at work full-time. The few who had failed to report were all recalled and made part of the recovery effort.

Specific objectives and time schedules were established to provide yardsticks for measuring recovery, a sense of real purpose and visible progress toward reopening. We met as a group each morning to review overall needs, plan daily actions and trade personal stories. These meetings provided a reassuring togetherness as well as common direction. Staff members brought ice, food and drinks for lunches, and a date for reopening—October 9—was set. The South Carolina State Museum generously sent a sizeable staff team to assist us for two entire days. Work priorities were determined and teams were established as appropriate. Age and physical condition helped to decide what kinds of work individuals could do, but everyone took part. Curators, for example, moved fallen tree limbs at our historic houses, administrators used chain saws and educators helped remove damaged fencing.

Although a simple thing per se, the last provided perhaps our single greatest common catharsis, a symbolic "pushing back" of Hugo's negative effects. A large wooden fence by one of our historic houses had partially fallen during the storm and constituted a hazard. Still, it resisted going down. Since we needed to fell it quickly, about 20 of us decided to force the issue. Director, gift shop clerk, curator, custodian and carpenter "heaved to" as one. After a lengthy time of dedicated pushing, it fell. When this happened, a great deal of frustration was released. That individual action, involving strenuous, tangible combined effort, helped to solidify an essential emphasis on succeeding by working together.

We tried to make the workplace as comfortable as possible. Everyone, naturally, wore work clothes for days. The museum's emergency generator provided electricity adequate for basic cooking, and this was a boon to those reduced to using camp stoves or propane grills in areas where electrical lines remained lifeless. When power was restored—far earlier than in residential areas—employees could take hot showers. This may seem like a small benefit. However, after a hard work day, with no electricity at home, it was high luxury.

To further confirm our common determination, we decided to press forward with our next scheduled special exhibition, whose completion had been thwarted by the hurricane. An opening date of November 16 was established. We were aware that few regular visitors would come to the museum for an indefinite period. Local residents were dealing with hurricane problems and tourists were few. The point, though, was that we would be open, that we would continue to accomplish previously established plans in addition to dealing with hurricane problems, and that in so doing we would contribute to the very necessary sense of community recovery. In sum, we retained a sense of organizational security and purpose.

To ensure that employees had time to care for personal problems, we established a reduced daily work schedule, increasing hours gradually as we approached the museum's reopening date. A principal concern among many was contacting their insurance adjustors. Given the magnitude of the damage, some were unable to do so until weeks after the storm. However, time off was provided—often at unavoidable last-minute notice—for meetings with adjustors and also for other personal needs.

A key factor to remember at all times, and particularly in a disaster situation, is that regardless of their dedication to the organization, employees will understandably give first attention to their homes and families. If these are secure, they can concentrate on the job. If they are not, work performance will suffer. Accordingly, we made every effort to ensure that employees were able to "secure the home front" while helping the museum recover.

Recovery continued despite ongoing distractions. Our telephone rang continually. "Experts" from without urged us to pay for them to come to Charleston to present public talks (and solicit clients) regarding repairing water-damaged materials. Reporters from other states and countries pursued stories about damage, consuming valuable staff time. "Conservators" offered assistance—for a price—and individuals tried to sell us expensive artifacts. Local seismic experts predicted that a major earthquake, more destructive than Hugo, could occur at any time. And—with the result of challenging staff morale further—the November 1989 issue of AAM's *Aviso* carelessly told our colleagues nationally that Charleston-area museums had not prepared for the storm. Such factors interfered with our work and helped keep stress at a high level. However, emphasis on firm objectives reduced their impact.

On October 9, we opened again for public visitation. We had few visitors for the remainder of 1989, and plywood-covered window walls awaited the replenishment of local glass supplies. However, there was a common sense of pride in having overcome tremendous challenges and once again resuming normal operations. Due to the large number of insurance adjustors, FEMA representatives and construction personnel from other states, few hotel rooms were available in Charleston into mid-1990. Tourism remained at an all-time low. Nevertheless, we were open for business.

Lessons Learned

It was soon apparent that some principal assumptions in our disaster planning required revision. We had done all we practically could to prepare for the storm. We had also responded well, in our opinion, to the post-hurricane challenges. Nevertheless, we found that we had emphasized preliminary readiness more than recovery, and that our working concept of "disaster" focused more on anticipating the event (i.e., the storm) than on mitigating its effects. In fact, the event produces the disaster and well-studied plans for recovery are essential. This being said, however, it must also be recognized that individual disasters provide peculiar problems which no plan can fully foresee. It is necessary to shun feelings of failure when the unanticipated occurs, for these can have only negative effect at a time when strong morale is imperative. Natural forces, we learned, may impose challenges far beyond those initially conceived—a recent case in point is the impact of the January 1994 Los Angeles earthquake on state-of-the-art freeway systems. Therefore, it is useful to consider even the most comprehensive plan as a detailed guideline whose actual implementation will require flexibility and improvisation. One must expect to encounter unforeseen problems and must not permit them to create self-doubt.

While stockpiling things such as food, water and basic supplies, we had assumed that at least some services, supplies and support would be subsequently available. This, however, was not the case. Damage was so severe and widespread that we were essentially on our own during the first few days after Hugo. Usually reliable contractors were engaged in other work; no plywood was to be found in lumber stores; police and National Guard troops were tied up in preventing looting. In short, we learned that we must henceforth plan to be as self-sufficient as possible in immediate post-disaster circumstances.

Another shortcoming was our assumption that all staff would be available—or at least reachable—as soon as possible to assist recovery. Most staff were able to report, but some had experienced extensive damage to or loss of their houses and others had been forced to take refuge in places other than those designated on the recall list. In addition, staff members necessarily had to ensure their families' well-being before returning to work. Although the majority soon made their situations known, we learned that there will be unavoidable delays in reconvening the workforce and that many, sometimes key, persons may be prevented from readily assisting recovery efforts.

We also found that some staff members simply remained unavailable for telephone recall, made no contact or just waited to be called. Needless to say, our revised plan emphasizes that, in the future, all staff must either report or make their situations known promptly. As was the case in preparation, post-disaster circumstances do not provide time for normal discipline. Those present went ahead with recovery work under adverse conditions. Interestingly, there was no recrimination. Productive staff simply filled the gaps and assumed responsibility.

The very important lesson of this was that the levels of responsibility, initiative and reliability demonstrated by individual staff members under normal operating conditions will not change but, rather, will be magnified in a disaster situation. Rank and pay level are irrelevant. Positive people will perform well in the worst of circumstances; others will give no more than marginal effort and probably less. Any staff deficiencies will only be exaggerated, not overcome. Accordingly, one can practically expect to depend upon a core of dedicated staff and to encourage participation from others.

The Director's Situation

Like everyone, the director must balance professional and personal responsibilities. Additionally (at least in a museum of this size), he must provide for the morale and well-being of museum staff and facilities, work with governing authorities, deal with relevant outside agencies and maintain a comprehensive perspective to ensure the organization's finances and future. This must be done while dealing with the myriad concerns that complicate the pre- and post-storm events.

The director should be present and visible to the greatest possible extent and share with staff in the extraordinary physical labor of immediate recovery. While inevitably receiving conflicting advice and information, he must be capable of making important decisions in an unsettled environment. All the while, he can expect constant questions, recommendations, advice and arguments from staff, complemented by calls from other agencies, inquiries concerning damage and time-consuming sessions with FEMA inspectors and insurance adjustors.

It is important that the director represent stability and control. He is, appropriately, the principal individual to whom board and staff members look for reassurance that the organization will be properly cared for. Recovery must never be in doubt, and both the notion and reality of unified effort must be emphasized. To this end, staff should be continually consulted in the problem-solving process and the board of trustees must be regularly informed. This helps to provide the essential framework of support necessary for productive leadership in all cases and particularly in times of crisis.

In truth, one's ability to perform effectively under adverse conditions depends largely upon his already established working relationships with staff and governing authorities. These do not essentially change when a disaster occurs. Although influenced by extraordinary circumstances, they remain basically constant. Accordingly, if a positive workplace is the norm, the director can expect support in overcoming problems. If not, inevitable differences in opinions, priorities and loyalties may have detrimental centrifugal tendencies.

Because our organization was sound, I received strong assistance from both board and staff following Hurricane Hugo. The board, for example, readily endorsed my recommendation concerning the use of reserve funds to support our employees and recovery. Staff, meanwhile, recognized that I was trying under unprecedented circumstances to do my best. They did not expect me to be all-wise. They did expect me to provide direction and support. In return, I expected and received their advice, assistance and full cooperation. Not all of my decisions were popular; indeed, some periodically countered individual staff priorities. Nonetheless, because of our history of positive interaction, they were supported and we continued to work as a team. The sound working relationship we had established prior to Hugo, then, was basic to our performance following the storm.

Communication with and concern for employees are also essential. The first is important because an informed staff is reassured, understands the overall status of things and can perform more capably. Staff meetings and personal conversations assisted this, while memoranda—sometimes several each day—kept employees informed and praised their progress. The second is significant from both a human and an operational standpoint. There may in fact be little one can do other than sympathize with a staff member. However, this alone is important. In our case, ensuring continued paychecks was an organizational sacrifice that employees appreciated. Also, due to personal acquaintance with a local power company executive, we were able to have electricity at our wildlife sanctuary restored far earlier than at other sites in the vicinity. This was a real relief for our caretaker and his family.

Board and staff members understand that the director has the same personal problems to care for as everyone else. Moreover, they recognize that he is attempting to deal with extraordinary events. Still, board members have their own individual problems and even talented staff with clearly delegated responsibilities can only partly compensate for a lack of positive leadership. It is therefore the director's responsibility to do everything possible to maintain general well-being in the workplace.

Summary

Natural disasters, like museums, take many forms. An organization's ability to deal with a crisis depends on a complex of factors including the peculiar situation of the institution and the kind and intensity of the disaster. This chapter has related the experience of a relatively small nonprofit organization with a major hurricane that affected almost the entire state. Individual circumstances, of course, determine appropriate responses. However, on the basis of what occurred here and in other local organizations during Hurricane Hugo, I believe that several observations are applicable to any situation.

General:

1) Include all relevant principal staff in emergency planning, and ensure that all staff are both familiar with the plan and know their respective responsibilities, thereby emphasizing collective responsibility and teamwork.

2) Attempt in emergency planning to anticipate worst-case scenarios, and have practice drills to identify areas for improvement.

3) Consider recovery preparation an essential priority in emergency planning.

4) Activate emergency plans as far in advance as necessary.

5) Prepare for self-sufficiency.

6) Anticipate the unexpected both in terms of events as well as human circumstances and reactions.

7) Regularly review and update emergency plans.

Managerial:

1) Realize that positive regular working relationships are critical to the organization's ability to accommodate a natural disaster.

2) Establish, through planning and staff training, as much predictability in the workplace as possible in preparing for and responding to the unpredictability of crises.

3) Be as precise as possible in designating pre- and post-disaster staff priorities and responsibilities.

4) Recognize from the outset that no plan can foresee all problems and that actual circumstances will require initiative and expedients. This is only realistic and will offset feelings of failure when contingencies arise.

5) Appreciate staff needs and concerns as part of emergency planning and response.

6) Expect individual staff characteristics to be exaggerated in a crisis situation.

7) Within the context of organizational needs and circumstances, be as supportive as possible of the staff following a disaster.

8) As quickly as possible following the disaster, establish schedules for recovery and emphasize future goals and objectives. Make the workplace an island of stability.

9) While taking time adequate to care for personal concerns, provide positive leadership.

10) Communicate and consult regularly with staff and governing authorities.

11) As recovery occurs, update plans to include lessons learned.

Conclusion

The actual business of repairing damages and restoring normal operations occupied the next several months. From the administrative standpoint, post-Hugo activities demanded a great deal of time over the next two years. However, instead of focusing upon these simply as problems, we incorporated them into regular activities and in several instances expanded the recovery efforts to accomplish previously planned improvements. Historic house repairs, for example, were combined with greater restoration plans that in one instance received an important award from the National Park Service. In short, we attempted, as possible, to employ the recovery needs as opportunities rather than as liabilities.

Despite the numerous personal and professional challenges that the hurricane presented, staff here continued to function in a basically normal fashion in the post-Hugo period. Although instances in the community of alcohol and drug abuse, psychiatric emergencies and domestic violence reportedly rose as a result of the storm, there were no substantive behavioral changes or problems among museum employees. Tourism, a principal income source for the museum, did not resume respectable levels until 1991, but this was to be expected and we accommodated it through budgetary planning. Those who were rebuilding or restoring damaged homes received preferred time off as required, but there was no abuse of this. Some staff turnover gradually occurred, but this was neither unusual nor the apparent result of hurricane-related difficulties. Indeed, most principal professional staff present in 1989 remain the same today.

From recovery operations to now, our focus has been on the positive, on the future. We have endeavored to avoid the not uncommon handwringing over "what might have been" or "what could happen next time." Yes, Hugo might have destroyed Charleston, but it did not. We could have a terrible earthquake like the one in 1886, but we have not. And yes, as annual newspaper retrospectives tell us, the "next storm may be worse," but we will deal with that when it happens. In the meantime, we concentrate on improving our operations. This includes, as might be expected, annual revision of our emergency plan. Updated to incorporate our Hugo experience, it is regularly reviewed and revised to try to ensure that we will be as prepared as possible should such a crisis happen again.

In sum, our experience was grueling—none of us wants to go through such a time again—but it provided an enhanced sense of mutual confidence and pride among both board and staff. Working together, we maintained The Charleston Museum as a viable, progressive organization. On the staff level, this attitude was confirmed by a casual remark a year after Hugo, when department heads assembled in my office to discuss the progress of Hurricane Lili, then heading toward Charleston. Although news media speculated that the storm, coming so soon after Hugo, might "deliver a knockout blow," the nervous atmosphere of such meetings in previous years was noticeably absent. It was now replaced by the calm observation and determination of veteran experience. As one senior curator noted, responding to my comment that we might have to implement emergency measures within the day, Lili was "only at 75 miles per hour" and, in any case, "we can do it again." I had always been proud of my staff and The Charleston Museum. At that moment, I was particularly so.

Part Two

Staff

The Unionization of the Exploratorium

The Exploratorium, San Francisco

Joseph G. Ansel, Jr.

On April 15, 1993, Goéry Delacôte, the Exploratorium's director, signed a contract that formally unionized the Exploratorium. While most of the Exploratorium's staff celebrated unionization as the successful conclusion of a 40-month struggle, others of us felt a profound uneasiness. Our place, the place Frank Oppenheimer named the Exploratorium, the place that originally couldn't even be described by a conventional term such as museum, had assumed an ordinary organizational structure.

The Exploratorium's modest beginnings gave no indication whatsoever of its future success and worldwide influence. On my first visit, I was struck by the incredible contrast between the pastoral exterior and the dark cluttered interior of the Palace of Fine Arts, the building where the Exploratorium has always been housed. Towering columns, capped by lintels and decorated with frieze work, and huge sculptures form a colonnade around a massive rotunda. This structure overlooks a pleasant lake and park. Behind this enormous Greco-Roman look-a-like is the building itself. While large, it remains an undistinguished structure made of steel and concrete. Inside, it looked to me in 1972 like a curved airplane hanger.

The early Exploratorium was mostly empty space. Dust from the constant exhibit fabrication covered everything. The office consisted of a used construction trailer that had been pulled into the building. Plastic sheeting protected the electronics shop from a leaky roof. Our graphics department amounted to small plywood shacks. A collection of donated power tools, federal surplus junk, battered army desks and a few stacks of purchased materials, all grouped haphazardly in one corner, constituted the exhibit shop. Some space filled with strange constructs—old trade show exhibits and interesting junk—was the exhibit floor. Temporary barriers of tattered, woven redwood screens blocked off empty space or cluttered "storage areas." There were a few interesting exhibits, but the only images from my earliest visit I can remember distinctly were the vivid, saturated colors created by Bob Miller's *Sun Painting*.

The staff was no more organized than the place, probably less so. There were 15 or 20 of us. Youth, energy and the immense freedom the place allowed, combined with the persistent and powerful vision of our brilliant, mercurial leader, held us together.

Nearly 20 years later, why would the staff of the quintessentially creative Exploratorium vote overwhelmingly for unionization? What benefits did they seek in union representation? Why did they want the union? What had we—management—done? How were things going to be different? And looking forward, what could be learned from the experience, and would unionization alter the Exploratorium's continuing creativity and future growth?

The Early Exploratorium

Before 1975, the Exploratorium's structure centered completely around the founding director, Frank Oppenheimer. If an organizational chart of that period ever existed, it might have looked like planets in orbit around a central sun. A large worn rug, dirty old couches and chairs formed the staff meeting area. Weekly meetings at which food was served were well attended. Communication could not have been more direct. Almost every staff member knew to some degree what others did. The boundaries between departments were weak. Indeed, the director himself used to build exhibits and even sweep floors. There were few titles, no organizational charts, and minimal separation between management and staff. Fluid cooperation among most departments was a matter of course. Exploratorium old-timers characterized this era by saying:

> "People had a lot of personal autonomy and people took a lot of personal responsibility without being assigned. . . ." There were "very ill-defined boundaries of one's job . . . ."

> "The staff was young and willful, bright and overqualified. There was no formal employee training. Certainly in my personal case there has been enormous opportunity for growth and change."

> "Frank was very strongly against rules. He would have as few rules as he could get away with."

> "It was anarchy and Frank was 'anarch.' People pretty much did what they saw fit within the purview of what Frank would allow."

Most staff expected to be consulted, they expected to have influence. This structure, with Oppenheimer in the center and everyone else arrayed around, left a legacy. In many cases staff saw their jobs as extending from minute technical details all the way up to helping set museum policy. While museum departments started to develop in the early 1970s and while a flat, but fairly clear, hierarchy also grew up, a family-like tradition persisted until the recent union drive. For example, until 1991 virtually any staff member who felt comfortable doing so could attend meetings of the Exploratorium's board of directors.

Notwithstanding these democratic trappings, the Exploratorium was never without firm management in the early years. Much of this management was effective and proper because it derived from Oppenheimer's vision and leadership.

> "It really was an endeavor of love and an expansion of consciousness. He engendered that in people. It was obvious that we were doing a great thing. I learned to trust Frank's intuition."

> "Frank was very good at getting people to share his belief."

When shared belief was not enough, Oppenheimer was also excellent at maintaining control by persuading his staff that they had really convinced him to do exactly the thing he intended to do at the outset. In retrospect, it is easy to see that Oppenheimer also usually made good decisions when it really mattered. And if an error occurred, Oppenheimer was excellent at justification after the fact and a master at playing one group against the other to neutralize all parties involved.

> "Frank would kind of pick people and get them fighting with each other, and I think he did that intentionally."

Despite Oppenheimer's machinations, his breadth, intelligence, charisma and incredible dedication, combined with occasional displays of genuine and beguiling charm, kept the Exploratorium's staff churning forward. He was simply unassailable as he struggled to teach the world a new way to educate.

Organic Growth

Starting with an initial grant of $50,000 from the San Francisco Foundation[1], the Exploratorium grew from an unknown upstart to a major institution in less than 20 years. With growth came change, and many people interviewed for this essay posit growth, with all of its implications, as an underlying cause of the eventual union movement. Communication became more difficult. With specialization, Exploratorium staff slowly lost touch with what others did. However, in these early years, growth also represented opportunity. In all interviews with long-tenured Exploratorium employees, no one can mention any formal employee training or development, save the opportunity to tackle any job that seemed remotely related to one's position at the time. Clerks became accountants and exhibit builders erected large buildings.

Basically, we assumed that we could do anything, and although somehow we knew this wasn't quite true, few core staff failed to try out different jobs. People's jobs evolved; therefore they often saw the institution's workings from different viewpoints. This reinforced their belief that they should have a say in and influence on museum-wide decisions. To understand this job-shifting, consider one Exploratorium employee who was hired in May 1974 to do exhibit maintenance. As time progressed, he became an exhibit builder, exhibit shop manager, chief designer for the exhibit sales program, an executive council member, and now is a unionized exhibit builder again.

This early system, with many generalists and few specialists, had advantages—fewer employees were needed and there was always plenty of work to do. Job responsibilities expanded to match interests. Few people were bored with their work and many employees made the Exploratorium the center of their lives.

With growth also came real supervisors, real departments, and eventually a real organizational structure. But it was the diagnosis of Oppenheimer's cancer in May 1983 that caused him to create the earliest version of The Exploratorium Staff Organizational Chart. This modest document was backed up by a Staff Distribution by Function and/or Area list. Well before Oppenheimer's death in February 1985, an executive council was in place that managed all areas of the Exploratorium. Departments grew too. Although there were earlier fund-raising officers, Virginia Rubin, the Exploratorium's director of development from August 1976 until the summer of 1986, succeeded in firmly establishing the Exploratorium's fund-raising group. Rubin's department was in some sense a prototype for others to come.

Although Oppenheimer had brought on a long string of prospective successors, he was never ready to cede power, causing these quite capable people to leave or be dismissed. Since Rubin had assisted in raising funds—the life blood of the place—and because she was decisive, she became acting director shortly before Oppenheimer's death and continued in this role for about two years. While she adapted to the spirit of the place, she also molded it. With the help of the staff, Oppenheimer's executive council, led by Rubin, kept the Exploratorium on track during the transition to new management.

Both the Exploratorium's early structure and organic inbred growth set the stage for a difficult period of conflict that ended in unionization. This same structure also produced a prolific outpouring of ground-breaking educational exhibits and programs throughout the 1970s and 1980s. I hope my brief characterization of that early time provides some background for the following. Below are factors that may be seen as underlying causes for the unionization of the Exploratorium.

Problems of Succession

Death of the Founder

Clearly Oppenheimer was not an ordinary museum director. He was the founder and the guiding light of the Exploratorium. As with any founder, a direct replacement was not a possibility. And anyone who followed would be compared with and judged against Oppenheimer, not an enviable position to assume. Moreover, Oppenheimer left to his successor a minimal endowment, unsure revenue streams, a physical plant that was desperately in need of complete renovation and expansion, quickly multiplying programs and institutional functions, and a very unusual organizational structure.

Multiple Leaders

In the six years following Oppenheimer's death, the Exploratorium had four different leaders: Virginia Rubin, Robert White, Robert Semper, and Goéry Delacôte. Two of these,

Rubin and Semper, were interim directors. Compare this to the preceding 16 years when Oppenheimer was developing the institution.

Continuity in Leadership

Continuity in leadership was lost when Rubin resigned after White's arrival on April 1, 1988. On May 1, 1988, Robert Semper took a one-year sabbatical. These departures left White without key executives who might have assisted him in the early months of his administration. The subsequent resignation of Bob Miller, Oppenheimer's senior counselor, some months later, deprived the Exploratorium of a spiritual leader.

Opposition to a New Director

In interviews many Exploratorium staff cited White's hiring as an extremely difficult time for the Exploratorium; the staff was almost unanimously opposed to his appointment. In the staff's eyes good credentials were insufficient for a new director; the comparison between the quixotic, brilliant Oppenheimer and the staid White was too great. While the Exploratorium's board of directors sought a director to build quietly upon Oppenheimer's success, the staff desired someone with vision and fire. White started work with so little support that his entire administration was difficult for all. In identifying White's hiring as the start of a difficult time, Exploratorium employees faced the fact that new people would be running the place. For the first time, many staff felt the sense of ownership Oppenheimer had inspired slipping away. They sensed the power of the Exploratorium's board of directors. Constant financial pressures made a bad situation even worse.

Staff Turnover

Three different chief financial officers served from 1985 to 1992, and three different directors of development also served during this time. Not just executives changed: the Exploratorium's development department was weakened by the turnover of five different development associates in this same period. One of these development staffers had written nearly $5 million of federal grants; the loss was felt. A feisty but talented director of operations left. Fourteen people ultimately left in layoffs. And the departures continued when Delacôte came on board. The entire accounting department, save one employee, resigned over spurious allegations of a breach of confidentiality. At least four controllers were hired and left in three years; two budget analysts came and went. Three key employees in the marketing division left and one marketing manager transferred to another division. The teaching programs lost a co-chairman of the Teacher Training Institutes.

The institutional memory of the Exploratorium dimmed, potential mentors had gone, and new hires stepped into a very strong institutional culture lacking an understanding of the true nature of the changes the Exploratorium was undergoing.

Constant Financial Pressures

In the winter of 1980, staff at the Exploratorium took a voluntary reduction in work hours and went on partial unemployment. While some employees were unable to accept less pay, the majority of the work force reduced hours dramatically. Members of the Exploratorium's electronics shop performed their jobs and then worked after hours for a local computer firm, Datapoint, to make ends meet. Other employees simply submitted time sheets reflecting half the hours they actually worked. Several managers, who were aware that we couldn't meet payroll, postponed receiving their paychecks until funds would be available. A substantial grant saved the day and the Exploratorium survived. About this time the Exploratorium's board began discussions on instituting an admission charge.

This crisis was perhaps the clearest example of the persistent financial pressures that plagued the Exploratorium. Many nonprofit organizations face similar pressures. Indeed, Thomas W. Leavitt, a former museum director, argues in an article in *Museum News* (May/June 1991) that financial insecurity may be a permanent problem for such institutions: "In the end, recessions may tend to accelerate the search for new sources of capital and operating funds. But the economic problems of museums are permanent and structural. That is the problem."[2]

Financial pressures in the winter of 1990 led to the first mass layoff in the Exploratorium's history. Without these financial pressures, the layoffs might not have occurred all at the same time, or in the same way, if they occurred at all. Without the layoffs, it is unlikely the Exploratorium staff would have organized.

Growth in All Elements

Organic growth fostered the Exploratorium's populist institutional culture, but by the late 1980s the institution simply suffered from expansion in nearly every area. There were more visitors, exhibits, programs, and staff. Budgets were higher: more money needed to be earned or raised. Mustering resources and managing staff both to expand and maintain existing operations became increasingly difficult.

Examples are easy to cite. With the need to charge admission in 1981, an entire admissions department had to be created. State and federal grant programs funded a wonderful new program, The Teacher Training Institutes, but this required more staff, new offices and somewhere to conduct additional classes. The number of accounting entries grew at a terrific rate and computer systems, both for general accounting and fund-raising purposes, were acquired. Indeed, computers sprouted up everywhere, and computer training and maintenance became a necessary function. A small film program began. Video facilities were donated and we began to make short videos. In 20 years the graphics department moved from creating handwritten exhibit labels to producing full-blown magazines and publications. Exhibits were being produced at the rate of 25 to 40 per year, and as these exhibits wore out, exhibit maintenance became a major burden. To make money, the Exploratorium created an exhibit sales division to reproduce and sell fancy exhibits.

The museum store doubled in size and was rebuilt or relocated three times. Food service expanded. A huge mezzanine was built and exhibit space shrank as huge trailers were dragged into the building to make marketing and development offices for the growing staff.

An Older Staff

The staff matured along with the institution. In the early years, the Exploratorium was unknown; its staff worked in a place that was "counter-culture" and financially insecure. We knew the Exploratorium could close its doors for any number of reasons in a fairly short time, but the staff were young, marginally paid, and not looking for lifelong employment. In my own case, I liked the job because of the near absolute freedom it afforded; we worked when we wanted and as long as we wanted. One year I worked nearly nonstop in the spring, summer, and fall, then skied 60 days during the winter. Security was of little concern and money was only important in a relative sense: you wanted to be paid fairly in relation to others.

By the late 1980s the picture was very different. Many staff had children and mortgages. After the high inflation years, living expenses were high and money was generally an issue for staff, as was job security. Although we realized we remained part of an incredibly successful experiment in education, some staff no longer had that sense of infinite possibilities. Moreover, long hours coupled with deadlines caused occasional staff burnout. This was surely the case after the creation of our first major exhibit sales project: the IBM show. When I crafted the Exploratorium's first pension plan in 1985, I spent days computing projected costs using detailed staff lists. In doing this, I realized that turnover had been low and that the average age of the core staff was rising. Job security was to be a key issue in the unionization drive.

San Francisco's Union Tradition

In an interview with Joann Jung, a union official, I asked if the San Francisco Bay area's union tradition had any influence on the Exploratorium's drive to organize. She replied that unionization might not have occurred if the Exploratorium had been located elsewhere. Jung noted the fact that unions generally do not arise where no union local exists to provide support.

Exploratorium staff had praise for Jung and others from the Service Employees International Union, Local 790A (SEIU Local 790A). Interviews with Exploratorium staff verified that the union organizers were skilled and sensitive. They remained good listeners, built support carefully and slowly, and evidently made few mistakes in orchestrating the staff's unionizing efforts. One earlier union drive around 1980 failed for two reasons: there was no groundswell of sentiment and union organizers failed to build support. Ten years later the Exploratorium's staff was committed and the union organizers more effective.

Effective Communications

Immediately after the layoffs, an internal memo from a staff advisory committee called for not just increased communication but more influence.

> "Staff, as well as Management, must become part of the dialog. It's all well and good to expect representatives to champion a cause, but Staff must knock on doors and give input and demand answers as part of their job. We can't always expect others to have the solution: we must go to the source and deal with the people directly involved with decisions."[3]

Direct, effective communication with the decision maker. This was what so many Exploratorium staff had in earlier years and still wanted; they saw it as part of their jobs. Another staff member described the early years in this way:

> "There was a court of last resort and that was Frank. And you could win the argument if you were right . . . he would tolerate dissent."

But even before Oppenheimer's death, institutional growth, staff turnover and a ragged organizational structure had begun to undercut informal channels of communication. Fewer Exploratorium staff knew what other staff actually did. As time passed, staff additions and replacements made it difficult to remember names and departments. Despite the proliferation of meetings, committees, memo trails and even e-mail, nothing worked quite right. New people often failed to socialize with the long-tenured staff. New managers arrived with a different view of organizational structure, usually derived from their previous jobs, and they were not always available to lower-level staff. One Exploratorium employee, who was to become a leader of the union movement, put it this way:

> "And the people who were being brought in to run the place, it was very, very clear that these

were not people who were going to run things the way that people were used to them being run, which was with some access to decision making. . . . You had a staff that was used to having a voice and there wasn't any place for that voice anymore."

Ron Hipschman, an employee who opposed unionization, put it this way:

"Disenfranchisement—The staff now feels as if it has no way to affect decisions concerning many financial, operational, managerial and philosophical issues even though those decisions directly affect them. Many decisions are made behind closed doors, in secret, without consultation with the staff."[4]

In interviews one Exploratorium first-line supervisor characterized management communication as "gratuitous." Old-time Exploratorium staff were amazed to discover secrecy used as a management technique. The separation between management and staff widened dramatically. A clash of cultures occurred.

The Proximate Cause

On November 27, 1990, the Exploratorium laid off 10 employees and reduced the working hours of nine others. If memory serves, these layoffs resulted in the departure of 14 of the 19 employees affected. Each of the 13 people formally interviewed for this chapter, including Delacôte and Jung, cited these layoffs as the proximate cause of the union drive. Other Exploratorium staff confirmed this view. As staff saw it, the layoffs marked a break in the trust that had developed over the years at the Exploratorium.

Many said it was not so much the fact of the layoffs but the way they were done. Process was critical and the legacy of involvement fostered at the Exploratorium magnified the shock of the layoffs. Exploratorium staff characterized the layoffs by saying:

"Certainly the rank and file of the institution had no say whatsoever in that process, I mean zero. . . . I think most people would say that. The process was an entirely top down one."

"The way the layoffs were orchestrated . . . they [management] used a strict corporate model . . . they [the departing] got a few words and an envelope and a pat on the back."

[Speaking of the layoffs and resignations in accounting] "It wasn't necessarily the actual events so much, or the actual results of those events. It was more the way that they were done."

"The staff realized that the place was not theirs anymore, that it was rapidly being taken from them. . . . The place will never belong to the staff again."

In writing this, there are so many memories and echoes. I recall that when Oppenheimer maneuvered me into undertaking some particularly onerous task, I argued with him, telling him that the Exploratorium was his place, not my place. He replied that the Exploratorium had been fashioned by so many different people and it was theirs. We were both right. Without him the Exploratorium would never have existed; without us believing it was ours, it would never have grown so. Of course, it was my place.

For many in management, it was our place, too. Certainly this was the case for Semper, the acting director during the layoffs. There was considerable anguish in the many executive council meetings that preceded the layoffs. We had no ill intentions. In retrospect, all we lacked were the right answers. In the late 1980s staff rarely faced directly the cold reality of finances. At the executive level, however, it is like your own checking account: Do you have the money in the account when the bills come due? Are you spending faster than you are earning? We didn't even have all the information we needed, because the accounting systems at the Exploratorium were hard pressed to keep up with the institution's growth and we had a new and inexperienced chief financial officer. We could not be certain of future revenue, and at the time there seemed to be no other alternative to cutting payroll. The question really came down to layoffs versus an across-the-board reduction in salaries.

Early in 1990 an organizational consultant was hired and substantial work was undertaken in long-range planning. The Exploratorium's management was trying to prepare for a new executive director; we wanted to provide an understandable starting place for a new administration. This consultant came well recommended, but had no previous experience with nonprofit institutions. She argued against across-the-board salary cuts, and felt it was better to take the one-time shock of the layoffs. In her view, the people laid off would recover and the institution would be better in the long run. New high-level Exploratorium managers who had been hired from the entertainment industry agreed. Moreover, the acting director was trying to build the organization. How could he hire new people and then immediately ask them to design their own pay cuts? And finally, if layoffs had to come, we did not want to push the task onto the new director who would arrive in February. The layoffs could taint the first days of his administration.

I managed to convince the executive council to suspend contributions to the Exploratorium's pension plan. This amounted to an across-the-board 3 percent cut for tenured employees but would not save all the money needed. The pension plan cut failed miserably in accomplishing a second goal: to convince staff that management cared and was in the same boat with them. No one noticed. After discussion, including some dissent, the decision to proceed with the layoffs was made. Few old-time employees on the executive council at the time could have felt comfortable. I surely did not. We were aware that museum-wide communication was a growing problem and that one particular committee, the policy committee, had never served well as the voice of staff to management.

At the same time, we were inundated with work and found it difficult to make the old informal communication work. I can recall trying to be accessible and spending hours listening to opinions and viewpoints; the conversations became exhausting. I could not change the decision to lay off staff. Moreover, I agreed that some positions were no longer needed and I wasn't free to speak of any particulars. Regardless of the financial squeeze, I believe that if we had known the layoffs were to result in unionization, we would not have made them.

The day before the layoffs were to occur, staff met offsite to discuss the situation. The next morning they posted a memo to the executive council that stated: "As Exploratorium staff we would like to negotiate a decrease in salary to prevent the impending layoffs." The memo had 50 names on it. When the layoffs occurred the following day, staff assumed we had ignored them and this made them feel all the more powerless and bitter. In fact, the decision had already been made.

Management attempted to carry out the layoffs properly. We received advice about this from our consultant. Each division head discussed the people who might be affected with their department head. Employee performance was obviously a criterion, as were the organizational changes that were underway. The actual decisions were made, or at least ratified, at the department level. The only exception was the one department head who was laid off. Warnings about the seriousness of the situation were provided, both in written memos and at meetings. For the first time at the Exploratorium, a fairly generous severance package, which included out-placement assistance (finding jobs for those laid off), was devised. While not every decision was unquestionable, and while not every action taken by management was perfect, given the fact that layoffs were to occur, management acted well. Most staff did not criticize the actual decisions; rather, they attacked their lack of input in the decisions.

What more could we have done to inform staff? Should we have let staff decide who would be laid off? Sincere concern for the unfortunate employees dictated that discussions be held in private. No division head felt general discussions about who might go were appropriate or tolerable. How could we possibly conduct such meetings? And whose job was this anyway, if not management's? How could any major layoff be other than top down?

The Aftermath of the Layoffs

Exploratorium employees simply could not accept that management made such decisions alone, even though this practice is routine in the business world. This went against the long-established traditions of the place. Management was no longer Oppenheimer. They didn't trust us as they had trusted him, and unlike him, we were ineffective in explaining our actions. Staff felt profoundly disenfranchised.

After the layoffs, employees who remained feared for their jobs. Much to my astonishment, this fear became apparent as I conducted interviews for this article. It was real, deep and pervasive. And staff bitterly resented new hires made after the layoffs, particularly when these people came in as management at high salaries. Due to high costs for severance and some rehires, the layoff saved much less than anticipated. This further embittered staff. Union organizing meetings began. These meetings were small at first and slowly grew to include the majority of the rank and file. Security was tight. Some staff felt they would be fired for organizing. This fear became a strong argument for a union contract, which would protect workers from arbitrary management action. Management would not have fired workers or even chastised them, but many staff feared it would. Only the most perceptive employees understood that there was nothing to fear:

> "The Exploratorium is a much more benevolent place than most. My general take on it is that management, compared to most institutions, was relatively enlightened . . . but that's an accent on relatively."

While such employees existed, we had totally lost the trust of the majority of the staff, and in several cases, management had lost the staff's respect as well. They no longer talked to us openly. They talked among themselves.

Still, there was one person who might have changed the outcome: Goéry Delacôte, who arrived as executive director enjoying broad support from the staff. He came from a French governmental organization, the Centre National des Recherches Scientifiques, where he had managed the dissemination of information concerning French scientific research. Avuncular, talkative and a bit exotic, Delacôte stepped into the Exploratorium's greatest organizational crisis ever.

Upon Delacôte's arrival the expectations of the rank and file varied. At the extreme, one staff member expected Delacôte to fire or demote managers who had participated in the layoffs; other staff I interviewed were much less demanding. There was a strong sentiment expressed in early organizing meetings that Delacôte should be given a chance. No one could blame him for the layoffs and absolutely no one interviewed did. The staff was bitter, but they still had hope. This grace period was not to last long.

Three Exploratorium staff interviewed mentioned a difficult staff meeting. Someone had anonymously broadcast an e-mail message correctly informing the staff of a large bonus one manager had recently received. Many felt the bonus was deserved and itself not the issue. However, at that time all salaries were public at the Exploratorium and the fact that the bonus was secret was an issue. Delacôte decried the anonymous nature of the broadcast and said he would not tolerate an attack on the individual who received the bonus.

The ominous part came when, according to staff interviewed, Delacôte suggested that if he discovered who the offending party was, he would ask him or her to leave. The rank and file took this as a threat and became fearful. Clearly the e-mail was anonymous principally because the sender feared retribution. This one comment fed the staff's fears and underlined their powerlessness.

The "secret bonus" was to figure in the union drive in three ways. Delacôte's comments at the meeting were the first; the fact of the bonus was the second; and accounting staff, upon demanding strict documentation before issuing a bonus check, felt themselves implicated as the source of the leak. For this and other related reasons, these three long-tenured accounting staff resigned in reaction. I spoke at length with all three at the time. And in trying to put a good light on these resignations, high-level managers including Delacôte were seen as glossing over the real nature of the departures. None of this was good, for several staff in interviews mentioned both the bonus and the accounting resignations as proximate reasons for the unionizing efforts. Further organizational decisions that came down from the top, coupled with the personalities involved on both sides, added to a mounting sense of disillusionment. Delacôte had had his chance.

In fairness, consider Delacôte's position. He faced all the problems of succession listed earlier and he remained under financial pressures that both limited his ability to move the Exploratorium forward and had the potential to force more reductions in staff. He was brand new to the place and knew neither the staff nor the community in which he was working. Upon Delacôte's arrival, the current head of the Exploratorium's development department resigned.

Nothing was particularly easy for this new director. Even before his hiring, Delacôte had established his plan to double or triple the physical size of the institution. He also wished to build upon a germinal media department and more-established teaching programs to create two new centers: The Center for Media and Communication and The Center for Teaching and Learning. So, in essence, Delacôte envisioned a publishing/media group and a mini-university as institutions related to the existing exhibition space, which was now called The Center for Public Exhibition. All of this would require money and a smoothly working staff. He had neither. Ironically, for those of us who bemoan the passing of the young Exploratorium, unionization may actually help the Exploratorium achieve these goals.

The Campaign, Election, and Contract Negotiations

Early in the morning of September 27, 1991, Joann Jung of SEIU Local 790A called

Delacôte to inform him that approximately 85 percent of eligible Exploratorium employees had signed union cards and that SEIU 790A had filed a union petition with the National Labor Relations Board (NLRB). Jung also asked that management recognize the union without a campaign and election and requested that contract negotiations begin forthwith. She characterized Delacôte's reaction as surprised but cordial. In talking with Jung, I sensed that she was a little surprised herself by Delacôte's pleasant demeanor, which she described as "warmer than most." Delacôte had worked in union organizations before and had even worked in a union organizing campaign in 1959. On the phone, the conversation ended with Delacôte suggesting he consult with his staff.

When Delacôte described the union petition to the executive council on October 1, 1991, he said that at first he thought it a good idea: The Exploratorium had strong leadership, so why shouldn't the employees have strong representation? We sat stunned. No one on the council openly supported unionization, although perhaps one or two present had some pro-union sentiments. In that meeting it was decided that at least the employees should vote the union in; they should have a choice and we should have a chance to lobby our position. To management's credit, no hint of retribution was considered; most likely, that fear was unjustified. The union was our fault. Management, both new and old, had failed to ensure a smooth transition after Oppenheimer's death. At the end of the meeting, Delacôte felt the staff should clearly express their choice in an election, and I believe he was right.

After that meeting, one newly hired executive naively expressed the sentiment that once the employees discovered what a union could and couldn't do, they would have nothing to do with it. My reply was that she had no sense whatsoever of the situation and that unionization was an extremely strong likelihood. The new hires didn't have a clue; they didn't understand that to get this far, a real change had occurred. Yet some of the new people would figure prominently in the contract negotiations that dragged on for months after the election. Honestly, other than to understand better the nature of the situation, the old-time executives didn't know what to do either. Few members of management had experience in union drives and none had anything like comprehensive experience. After that first meeting, I predicted we would have a union. The organization had outgrown its earlier familial structure, yet the staff's need for direct involvement, which developed over nearly 20 years, had never been addressed adequately. So many I interviewed said the union drive was about a balance of power. We had ignored or taken away their voice, and the union was the only way staff felt they could get it back.

The campaign that preceded the election had two notable occurrences: the NLRB debates, and staff attempts to create a staff association.

The Exploratorium hired an attorney to conduct seminars for management and to help us convince employees that a union was not in their best interest. I attended these seminars and received copies of the NLRB regulations that constrained our actions during the upcoming campaign: we could not interrogate, threaten, spy on or make promises to rank-and-file employees. The lawyer made it clear that if we did nothing, the union would win the election. He also said that the union would draw a clear line between the rank and file and management; about this he was right.

Owing to charges that the attorney was a union-buster, the staff insisted that he should not continue to advise management. The Exploratorium's regular law firm, Cooper White and Cooper, took his place. A few days after notification, Delacôte had already decided that the employees should have the chance to vote and the executive council agreed. The union succeeded in using against us the fact that we had hired an experienced labor attorney. Amazing. None of this was pleasant; tensions grew. Cooper White and Cooper held no seminars and I can recall no further advice being offered as to how we could convince staff that a union was not right.

There were two NLRB-sanctioned debates at which members of the staff who usually were quiet and unassuming spoke eloquently and from the heart about why unionization was necessary. I was amazed to learn who the leaders of the movement were. Most of them had over 10 years at the Exploratorium, and I began to see unionization was not about wages or even fundamentally about the fear the layoffs had engendered. Rather, it was about power over the place they had helped to create and still wanted to manage. And it was about respect and trust. Management did not do well in the debates.

Exploratorium staff who opposed the union struggled for an alternative, and on November 18, 1991, Ron Hipschman and Pat Murphy issued an 11-page memo proposing a staff association modeled on a similar employee group at the California Academy of Sciences, a nearby natural history museum. Members of the California Academy of Sciences staff association came and described their association in a well-attended meeting held shortly after the memo was issued. It became clear that the California Academy of Sciences staff association was working well and had one absolutely essential feature a union would lack—it was all-inclusive. It would not separate management and staff. Such an association produced a contract that was binding on the executive director. And finally, the association secured one seat on the board of directors, so staff were directly represented at all meetings. Essentially, such a staff association amounts to an all-inclusive, self-managed union, with a legally binding labor contract, board representation and no union dues. Union organizers opposed this idea. From their point of view, it was a very dangerous idea, came too late and would be subject to manipulation by management. At least one proponent of the staff association was accused of being a pawn of management, which definitely was not true since management saw the whole business as skirting on unfair labor practices and sanctioned none of it. An opportunity was missed with the staff association.

The union won the election overwhelmingly. All that remained was the contract.

Everyone agreed that contract negotiations took too long. Initial talks started in May and the group really got down to business by July 1992. Gregory Lim, the union's lead negotiator, had immediate praise for members of the Exploratorium's council of stewards and he emphasized their patience. They worked toward an agreement that provided unusual flexibility and which, to the best degree possible, maintained the Exploratorium's creativity. I believe everyone was concerned with the Exploratorium's well-being, but management seemed less sure of itself in the negotiations. Sherry Rodgers, director of operations and human resources, characterized negotiations as immediately very adversarial and confrontational; it was her first union negotiation.

Eventually both parties wore thin. Toward the end of the negotiations, one Exploratorium steward described the negotiations as "extremely frustrating—incapacitating." To prod the Exploratorium forward in negotiations, the Exploratorium staff had a "sick-out" and conducted informational leafleting. Strike sanction was also secured from local unions. And although absolutely no one wanted a strike, people began to talk of the possibility. Late in negotiations Semper assumed negotiations for management and began to move the talks forward. Lim credits Semper with working honestly to a "meeting of the minds" that resulted in an agreement after a 30-hour negotiating session on March 1, 1993. The Exploratorium had a contract.

Two individuals I spoke with about unionization expressed the opinion that all organizations, once they reach a certain size, benefit from unionization. Not surprisingly, these views came from a union official and one particularly thoughtful union organizer at the Exploratorium. Their reasons were different. Jung believed that no matter how benevolent management might be, it could change, and once it changed workers would eventually be denied the working conditions and benefits they deserved. She also felt "the issues are always there" and a union contract addresses and resolves those issues effectively. The Exploratorium organizer spoke more philosophically of democracy:

> "As a general principle I believe in some sort of genuine democratic control by workers over many of the essential, particularly economic aspects of work."

And although Delacôte would have preferred a staff association, he viewed unionization as part and parcel of the normal development of the Exploratorium. Speaking of unionization, he said, "Again, I don't think it is a dramatic evolution. Oh, no, not at all."

While democratic management is best, my own belief about unionization, both its desirability and inevitability, is different.

Fundamentally, the union divides the staff between the bargaining unit and management. Union supporters point out that this division arises from labor-law provisions, but the fact that the law mandates the division does nothing to alter the nature of the division itself. No amount of arguing can obscure the fact that the union contract applies only to the bargaining unit; it only protects and represents a percentage of those who work at the Exploratorium. Having split the parties, the union leaves one third of the employees without whatever assistance the union can afford. Many staff expressed sorrow that the union was necessary, thus tacitly, or even explicitly, acknowledging the rift unionization would create.

The fact that a third party—the union itself—oversees discussions between these two groups works to define the relationship further. It is a tripartite relationship that easily inclines all parties toward competitive rather than collaborative negotiation; clearly this was the nature of the Exploratorium's contract negotiations, at least until the final stages.

In unionization lies the risk that the Exploratorium's creativity, spontaneity and even efficiency will suffer. Many of the clichés about union shops have some grounding in reality. For example, seniority is probably not the best way to rank and judge employees, and while the union exists to protect workers, at times workers may take advantage of this. With the union now in place, staff, management and the union itself must guard against such things.

The union has its own agenda too: it exacts dues from the workers and creates a closed shop. While sitting in SEIU's large but scruffy offices, you do not have the impression that SEIU 790A is looking out for its own interests. The brightly colored mural behind me— created in a Diego Rivera fashion—bespoke of working people's battles. Both union officials I spoke to impressed me with their quiet, sincere dedication to their cause. At the same time, these outsiders were installing an artificial structure on the place that so many others and I had fashioned. The Exploratorium is still relatively small, with perhaps 150 full-time equivalents employed. Did we really need the union's help? How had we abused our workers so?

Wages and benefits at the Exploratorium remain very good, and Jung agreed with me when I mentioned this fact. All these benefits, including six weeks of paid vacation for long-tenured employees, were initiated long before unionizing efforts began. The union's traditional role as guardian of abused workers didn't match the facts. There was no corporate greed at the expense of the workers. Precious few at the Exploratorium could be considered ill paid or economically abused.

The Exploratorium's union drive was about respect, trust and power. Management and staff failed to foster respect and trust. And management failed to create channels of communication that would provide adequate influence and power to employees, many of whom simply loved the institution. I cannot say if the staff expected too much, but only that their need for involvement clearly matched their dedication.

Management, eventually led by Delacôte, had desired a formal organizational structure. In crafting this structure, management failed to accommodate the needs of the Exploratorium's staff. Before unionization, certain key managers, often newly hired, expressed views such as "we can't go on like this" or "we are good at creating, but not managing." My reply on one occasion was that the Exploratorium had become world famous and immensely successful by being different, not by taking the common route. The new managers had little sense of what had made the place great. The familial structure had worked under Oppenheimer, and Rubin's administration had begun a transition to a management structure more suitable for the maturing Exploratorium. A solution that would unify rather than divide staff would have been the proper way to build on the Exploratorium's tradition.

What Can We Learn from the Unionization of the Exploratorium?

My opinions and observations in this section are just that. In learning from the Exploratorium's experience I assign no blame; it does no good.

Management is not a science—not at all near a science. At times I wonder if it is even a discipline. (Read Neil Postman's *Technopoly* for a different viewpoint on the social sciences.) What we learn, and think we understand, may not apply to a different situation. We can learn from a novel, or a story, or from careful observation of the facts around us, as well as from a textbook. With management this may be the better route since so many trendy management theories come and go. *The Wall Street Journal* acknowledged this in a front-page story with the column heading: "The Best Laid Plans: Trendy Management Schemes Very Often Fail; Still Firms Keep Trying Them Out."[5] Plus, personalities figure into management, which makes management all the more complex. Nevertheless some general concepts are clear. Management without leadership translates into power without guidance. And leadership without wisdom and vision takes us to the wrong place.

First we can learn that unions may arise in relatively small and highly creative organizations. Who would have expected the Exploratorium's staff to organize? No longer think of unions as appropriate to the manufacturing sector only. There are a number of reasons for this:

1. Service industries are where the workers are, and unions know this. According to Jung, unions are actively moving into the service sector—including nonprofits.

2. As the Exploratorium shows so well, not all union drives are about bread-and-butter issues. Simply because an organization pays well is no guarantee that it satisfies all of the

essential needs of its workers. Indeed, once primary needs are satisfied, secondary ones become important.

3. Small, highly creative institutions contain a high percentage of employees who are capable of leading a union drive or carrying it forward. It takes only one person to suggest the idea.

Perception can serve as reality. Delacôte noted that much of the Exploratorium staff's fear was unjustified by the facts. While this point can be argued, the fear was real, justified or not. And it served as a real motivating factor in unionization. Feeding this fear in any way, such as in the staff meeting mentioned earlier, was a clear mistake. Ironically, because the fear exists, five positive comments are required to mitigate one negative comment. For reasons of survival, people who fear are selective in their perception of the facts. Although Oppenheimer allowed staff to have substantial power, he also created the illusion that they had more influence than they actually did. In this he used their perceptions to his own ends. Issues of higher morality aside, at times it worked.

Management's attempts to "move on" or "put the situation in its best light" failed miserably after the layoffs. While we were moving on, the staff was organizing. Glossing over the facts and ignoring past traditions didn't work. Several staff, years after the fact, could describe in fair detail the going-away party for the three accounting staff who resigned. In interviews I could taste their bitterness when they recalled management suggesting at the party that the departing employees were "going back to school." Such memories are like the fear mentioned above. It doesn't matter if they are correct or not, they are real for those who carry them. Address the facts and deal with the facts—nothing else will do. Recognize and attempt to resolve honestly important issues first and then move on.

If you are going to move on, it helps to have means and something to move on to. Both financial pressures and organizational turmoil, combined with unclear directions for the future, made it nearly impossible for many staff to find new pleasure in their work. Under these circumstances "moving on" really doesn't work. Due to lack of funds, some simply didn't have much work. For example, the video program—an important element of The Center for Media and Communications—was limping along with little funding. Few mission-oriented employees at the Exploratorium enjoyed the expansion of the museum's marketing efforts, notwithstanding the fact they sometimes understood the need. So marketing, which was expanding, was not usually a place the mission-oriented people would gravitate toward. Moreover, while many creative staff expressed pleasure with Delacôte's new general topic of cognition, they found little indication from management as to how to exhibit this topic. Cognition is an internal mental process that does not fit nicely into the Exploratorium's principal exhibition modality: interactive table-top exhibits. Compare this to Oppenheimer, who occasionally employed a highly effective technique to lead a new exhibit program—he would build such a junky prototype exhibit that skilled staff would rebuild the thing so that it really worked.

Oppenheimer wrote, "In talking about exhibit design, I want to avoid a propensity that frequently plagues discussions about teaching, namely telling people how to teach without any reference to what they are teaching." The underlying principle that Oppenheimer employs in this quote applies to managing as well as teaching. Abandon the myth of generic managers, at least for small- or medium-sized organizations. While professionalism, new ideas and new input are vital, it helps immensely to know a great deal about the work of those you manage. I agree with Admiral Rickover, who in a speech at the Columbia School of Engineering stated:

> "Many who teach management in our universities do their students and society a disservice. By focusing on the techniques of 'modern management' they promote the idea that by mastering a few simple principles of how to handle people and situations one can become a universal manager: capable of running any job without having to know much about the work being managed."

In an attempt to reinvigorate management, we hired people lacking experience in nonprofit educational settings. Moreover, due to staff turnover, organizational turmoil and a very weak tradition of internal employee development, there were never effective mentors for these new hires. Understanding their situation and adapting were real problems for them.

Attend to the communication function and allow for genuine input. The Exploratorium's democratic traditions made providing staff a measure of influence essential. In describing the difficulties of communication, Exploratorium staff often refer to a committee that was initially called the Policy Committee. This committee consisted of members elected by the staff, as well as members appointed by the director. It was supposed to provide staff input on important issues. Management had neither the time, nor later the inclination, to make this committee work as intended. Eventually, almost no staff chose to run for positions on the Policy Committee. Changes in the name of the committee reflected its reduced role: The Policy Committee became the Policy Advisory Committee. In the end, the very existence of the committee served as a constant reminder that staff's power was declining. If management fails to share power, the staff might take what power it can.

In meeting after meeting, management admonished its members to inform staff of its decisions. The formulas went something like this:

1. Best was to take input before the decision was made and then to act on that input.

2. Second best was to take input and then do otherwise, but with clear indications staff have

been heard.

3. Third best was to take action and explain to the staff after the fact.

4. Unacceptable was to say nothing.

All of this is good, but what usually went unsaid is, when it really matters, the decision must be correct. We made some wrong decisions and we compounded this by not recognizing them and correcting them. Once staff decide a decision is both important and wrong, you either have to convince them that you did the right thing or you must accept that you did not. To do otherwise gives the staff little confidence that you will decide correctly in the future when it really matters. They will no longer trust you to exercise your power well.

In developing the institution, foster formal and informal staff development. Staff members at the Exploratorium often had opportunities, but they rarely had mentors or more conventional training. While new people bring fresh ideas, talent and energies, long-tenured employees will be sensitive to the traditions of their organization and capable of helping new people fit in. If hiring from without, seek employees who understand nonprofits and mission-oriented organizations. The business world is different and few truly understand both worlds.

Finally, if staff seem to need a voice, if current systems for staff influence are failing, consider a staff association. Although, regrettably, recent NLRB rulings[6] outlaw such associations in a union shop, a staff association has several features to recommend it. Both a staff association and a union can produce a contract that constrains management and also defines very clearly the staff's power. There is nothing illusory about such contracts in either case; they are binding on both parties. But a staff association has advantages over a union. A staff association can:

1. Define itself as a legal entity to negotiate a binding contract.

2. Include all employees except the executive director.

3. Draw no line between management and staff.

4. Introduce no third parties into either contract negotiations or contract administration.

5. Secure representation on the institution's board of directors.

6. Create an elected position to directly represent the staff in all executive meetings so that the staff are both informed and have a day-to-day say in the management of the place at the highest level.

7. Address a much broader set of issues, including issues that would fall completely under management's purview in a union shop.

8. Convene a staff council that would initially negotiate a contract with management and then hold monthly meetings of all the staff to discuss ongoing concerns.

9. Operate within the contract.

10. Represent the staff in binding arbitration, or litigation, with the director if contract terms are violated.

11. Secure a budget from the institution to operate. Charge no dues to members.

The advantages are obvious and compelling.

Now that the union is a fact at the Exploratorium, how have things changed?

Many employees expressed the opinion that the union had little effect on the Exploratorium, that management's actions over the transition years, and Delacôte, had changed the Exploratorium—not the union.

But one thing is clear: the fear is gone. No bargaining unit member I approached had the least compunction about speaking to me. Interestingly enough, this was not the case with management; several managers shied away from commenting and one manager spoke to me only on the condition of complete anonymity. Managers are aware that they can be disciplined for speaking their views, although most probably simply wanted to forget the whole unionization issue and move on.

People are less engaged with their work at the Exploratorium. Shortly before unionization, I was absolutely astonished to hear one newly hired employee describe her job as: "It's just a job, like any other job." Growth, maturation of the staff, employee burnout or even focused job descriptions could all be a cause of such feelings. Yet, I doubt the union or restructured management will succeed in engendering the highest levels of commitment from staff. Many staff now feel strictly limited in influence. On the good side, there may be more balance in employees' lives; those early days of wildly working were a bit self-destructive, exciting as it was.

While it is too early to say if unionization will contribute to the overall happiness of the Exploratorium's employees, there is reason to doubt that this will be the case. A research group, the Center for Value Research (CVR) of Dallas, has conducted studies over the years of unionized and union-free organizations. CVR conducted a survey of employee attitudes in 113 companies. The total number of employees polled was 45,498 and legitimate statistical techniques were employed in the study. The results are summarized by the quote below:

> "Union leaders have always claimed that joining a union will make employees happier

because it will provide them with better pay and benefits, more job security, less favoritism and more consistency. Study data clearly show that union employees are not more satisfied than union-free employees; they are less satisfied. This holds true regardless of age, sex, race, length of service or education."

An immediacy has been lost. Staff now talk of endless budgeting and paperwork. Interdepartmental communication and approvals take time. Some strict work schedules now exist, and hours for nonexempt staff are strictly limited. Formal communication channels established in some departments require old friends to communicate through others. Staff meetings are held four times a year instead of four times a month. I am not in a position to attribute such changes to the union; much of this may simply be the result of growth. However, at the executive level, the union requires substantial time. Sherry Rodgers, who was responsible for human resources at the Exploratorium, reported that 80 percent of her time was consumed by union matters during contract negotiations and that a great deal of her day was still consumed by union affairs after the contract.

On the positive side, the Exploratorium continues to adapt and change; it is building an organizational structure that may allow it to undertake substantial work Oppenheimer could never complete. Oppenheimer was interested in creating a new way to educate and he wanted to teach the world what he had learned. In this he succeeded. And to undertake such work Oppenheimer required a particular type of highly flexible, fast-moving organization—the early Exploratorium. The Exploratorium faces new and different challenges now. For example, the physical plant, which Oppenheimer ignored, remains altogether unsuited to housing a major educational institution. A new organizational structure, in part arising from unionization, may help in undertaking such tasks as the expansion and renovation of the Exploratorium's home, the Palace of Fine Arts.

The union has begun to show potential as a forum for handling all the various complaints and problems that any active institution encounters; it does represent the staff to management. And this particular union, SEIU Local 790A, seems particularly sensitive to the Exploratorium's history, traditions and current needs. Moreover, many Exploratorium staff are convinced that the present leaders at SEIU Local 790A operate with an admirable moral sense. In my short interviews with union staff, they seemed to be fine people. This gives me hope that much of what I value in the Exploratorium will survive and prosper.

One staff member asked me not to write this essay. I hope he errs in worrying that the tone of this chapter is wrong or that it will hurt the Exploratorium. Although I could tell the story of the union drive, he argued, no ending to this story exists, and it is too soon to discuss the effect of the union on the Exploratorium. With this I agree. But what really resonated in me, as he spoke, were the words below. They are his words, but I take them as mine to end this chapter.

"It's a place that has had a huge impact on my life personally . . . and you know, I love the place and I care deeply about it and it's still very important to me. To me it still has a tremendous amount of its original spirit. . . . The reason I'm sitting here doing this is because I care about the place."

Footnotes

1. Hilda Hein, *The Exploratorium: The Museum as Laboratory* (Washington: Smithsonian Institution Press, 1990), p. 18.

2. Thomas W. Leavitt, "Permanent Problem?" *Museum News,* American Association of Museums, Washington, D.C., May/June 1991, Vol. 70, No. 3, p. 59.

3. Internal Exploratorium Memo, Policy Advisory Committee Response to the Museum Restructuring, D. Barker, J. Bell, K. Finn, C. Greene, R. Meyer, December 10, 1990, p. 6.

4. Internal Exploratorium Memo, Proposed Staff Association, R. Hipschman, P. Murphy, November 11, 1991, p. 6.

5. Fred R. Bleakley, "The Best Laid Plans," *The Wall Street Journal,* Western Edition, Vol. CXXIX, No. 3, July 6, 1993, p. A1, A6.

6. Kevin G. Salwin, "DuPont Is Told It Must Disband Nonunion Panels," *The Wall Street Journal,* Western Edition, Vol. CXXVIII, No.109, June 7, 1993, p. A2.

The Illness and Death of the Chairman

American Museum of Natural History, New York

Marcia White and Talbert Spence

I n January 1992, Dr. Malcolm Arth, chairman and curator of the Education Department at the American
Museum of Natural History, died at his home in Manhattan. According to *The New York
Times*, "[Dr. Arth's] relatives said he died after a long illness." No other details of his illness
were released publicly.

Dr. Arth was widely respected as an anthropologist and educator. He was an innovator,
a skillful fund raiser, an advocate for multiculturalism and was at the forefront of museum education reform for 20 years. During his career, with wit, sensitivity and scholarship,
he published many articles in anthropology and museum education journals, sharing
developments of the heralded programs he nurtured at the museum. Two extraordinary
legacies of his talent are the world's foremost anthropological film festival, The Margaret
Mead Film Festival, and the People Center, a facility in the museum that showcases the
cultural anthropology of both little- and well-known societies through intimate-format
lectures, films and dance performances. Dr. Arth was a global leader in museum education, which gave him opportunities to work with and advise many museums and cultural
groups. He particularly enjoyed working with older adults, a special research interest of
his. He taught regularly at New York University in the Anthropology Department and at
the internationally respected Getty Trust Museum Management Institute in California.

The issue of illness as a life crisis for a colleague, his family and professional associates
has been given inadequate attention in the museum community. Dr. Arth was ill for a
period of at least five years prior to his death. Some of those who worked closely with him
felt that he suffered greatly, both emotionally and physically during this time. Dr. Arth
made the decision not to admit openly to the staff that he was ill or to prepare them fully
to take over his major responsibilities. This created a barrier between him and the department staff who needed help coping with his and their emotional upheaval caused by his
illness, and the change that was forced upon them.

Change

Change is a very complex and difficult endeavor for individuals and groups, even without
living through the emotional fallout of the terminal illness of a respected leader.
Associated with such an upheaval are a flood of entangled emotions including anger,
bereavement, fear, vulnerability, relief and uncertainty about the future. In the Education
Department at the American Museum of Natural History, such a change occurred. The
web of feelings that accompanied this change was apparent in the museum's Education
Department with the onset of Dr. Arth's debilitating illness and subsequent death.

An organizational change accompanied this personal tragedy. It began in 1988 with the
museum going through a transformation of its top administrative leadership, the intro-

duction of new administrative practices and the redefinition of the institutional mission, goals and objectives. This new management structure was welcomed, and has proved to be effective. A commonality of goals that transcends the different loyalties of the museum's subunits is now accepted and recognized as part of the effort to bind the institution together.

The position of vice president for public programs was created during this period, and represented a significant structural change. The goal was to coordinate the public program subunits and thus improve internal communications, as well as administrative and program development practices. However, the interface between the curator and chairman of the Education Department and the new vice president for public programs was not successful, and one result was a seriously strained relationship. There was a feeling among senior staff of the Education Department that the side effects of this strained relationship affected the view that the senior administration had regarding the loyalty of the chairman of education to their mission, as well as the participatory role the Education Department played in the museum's public programs and the decision-making process in developing exhibition projects. The combination of the museum's organizational reforms and the illness of the chairman created a stressful work environment where the web of emotions grew with great intensity.

Karen Wilhelm Buckley and Dani Perkins suggest in their essay "Managing the Complexity of Organizational Transformation" from *Transforming Work* (Miles River Press, 1984) that "within a major change, a transformation may or may not occur, depending on the readiness and willingness of the individual or the organization. Transformative change is accompanied by a fundamental shift in consciousness, values, or perceptions. This level of change entails a profound transmutation of the prevailing vision of reality. This shift in consciousness alters the basic ways an organization or individual responds to the environment. A transformation has occurred when new meaning is successfully established in relation to the organization's environment."

Change is ongoing and unavoidable in organizations and in our personal lives. It sometimes comes with the realization that things are not working well. This can bring a degree of discomfort, but in the best of circumstances, a tension-filled situation may evolve to an action state that is challenging, exciting and ultimately comfortable as the change settles in. Whether the transition is developed internally or imposed from an outside source, organizations and individuals may find themselves experiencing the same type of turmoil.

Trust

Management styles vary depending upon the personality, training and work experience of the particular manager and the accepted management system within the organization. Dr. Arth's style was widely acknowledged as one of absolute control of all operations and decision making, allowing only the most rudimentary issues to be handled by others. He was not inclined to befriend staff inside or outside the museum, nor was it natural for him to express warmth toward them. He was a fiercely private individual who carefully guarded the details of his personal life, which he never discussed with his staff. He also did not believe that personal situations in his or his staff's lives should be allowed to affect their performance and judgment in the workplace.

Maintaining this personal philosophy may have been a factor in how Dr. Arth dealt with the stress and trauma caused by his illness. Because he had never developed a warm, personable and mutually trusting relationship with his staff, he was unable to reach out to them when he became ill. At the same time, those who were aware of his illness found it difficult to approach him about the topic and to express their concern. This dilemma not only had consequences for the staff, but came to jeopardize some of his many accomplishments within the museum. During the advanced stages of Dr. Arth's illness, important museum policy information was not shared with the key managers, and his vigorous advocacy of programs, staff positions and even the acquisition of equipment and materials was absent.

The reasons for Dr. Arth's actions during this immensely stressful time are undoubtedly complex. One can only speculate about them. Was it perhaps that, in his mind, passing on important information and relinquishing many of his key duties implied losing control at the museum? Was his reluctance to share power based in part on his fear of losing the personal battle against his illness? One can easily sympathize with a person who might need to assert even greater control over his professional life if he felt that he was losing control of his personal life and well-being. Indeed, each of us might easily do the same in a similar situation.For Dr. Arth, the part of his personality that allowed him to flourish in the professional spotlight and to assert control in his areas of expertise also drove him to be a prolific writer, a charming host at social occasions and an excellent consultant. He was adept at isolating issues and problems and fixing them. On the other hand, he did not strongly encourage staff to collaborate freely with him at his own level or to develop professionally. Often his attitude could be summed up as "my way or the highway." This point of view effectively tied the hands of those who worked with him, and caused a great deal of frustration and ultimately anger among the managers of the department and the other staff.

When well, Dr. Arth was always a take-charge manager and a powerful advocate for the Education Department's policies with the administration. His colleagues who knew him outside of the museum admired his strengths and passionate ideas. He traveled extensively as a museum consultant and as an anthropologist. Whenever he traveled he was in contact with his office; we always knew how to reach him.

As we began to suspect he was ill, however, we realized he would neglect to leave a means of contacting him when he traveled abroad. This was not his regular working pattern. There was private speculation that this unusual behavior may have been connected to his receiving medical treatment abroad prior to its approval by the Federal Drug Administration in the United States. But because everything surrounding Dr. Arth's illness had to be kept virtually secret, none of the staff's concerns could be expressed openly, and no direct questions could be asked.

Over time, as Dr. Arth became increasingly ill, important issues that affected the smooth running of the department were not addressed with the same speed and determination as in the past. Sometimes, uncharacteristically, it appeared that he could not make a decision, and yet he would not let us make the decision without him unless we insisted. It became increasingly difficult for him to fulfill his outside consulting responsibilities and he began to cut back. On occasion, he did not give explanations for a cancellation or his failure to keep appointments. As a result, the managers under his supervision were faced with the responsibility of tying up loose ends, while at the same time protecting his privacy concerning the illness. All of this must surely have been confusing to the outside museum community.

Under the personnel policy of the American Museum of Natural History, an employee who spreads malicious gossip can be terminated from his position. Since Dr. Arth never admitted that he was suffering from a terminal illness, discussing his failing health openly could have been dangerous to an individual's job security. Therefore, the managers and staff were very careful about what they said to the administration, to other departments within the museum and particularly to outside organizations. We all walked on eggshells. This only added to our stress.

Throughout this difficult period the Education Department's program managers, with minimal assistance from the vice president for public programs on major policy issues, proceeded in Dr. Arth's absence to conduct business with outside clients and to conduct exceptional programs for school groups, adults and families.

It is our belief that the adherence to museum protocol by senior museum management, and the lack of responsive personnel policies to support employees in situations of this nature, may unintentionally have contributed to morale problems and emotional trauma among the department's staff. The chairman's illness and its impact on his staff were officially ignored at the same time that preparations were being made for Dr. Arth's retirement.

Staff Survival

Dr. Arth did ask the administration to establish an independent outside assessment committee, known as the Visiting Committee, made up of museum colleagues. The committee was to evaluate the department and its interaction with other museum departments, and to recommend a direction for the future after Dr. Arth's retirement. After he became ill, Dr. Arth decided to retire, but did not announce the official date.

The Visiting Committee conducted its evaluation in the winter of 1990. The committee read background material, interviewed staff for two days and wrote an evaluation. Although Dr. Arth had been adamant that this evaluation should take place, he was not pleased with the resulting report. Senior museum management decided that they would take no action recommended in the report until a new chairman was in place.

Despite the gesture of an independent evaluation, there was a great deal of anger among the department staff, from assistant chairman down to the support staff. The anger was targeted primarily toward Dr. Arth's inability to trust us and allow us to share in the trauma of his illness. But there was also resentment that he was not adequately helping us plan for the transition and ultimately the major change that would come with his loss. We were angry, too, at the illness for changing him, for putting added responsibilities on us, for leaving us powerless to make decisions, comfort him and move forward.

The department managers attempted to shield the staff from problems resulting from Dr. Arth's changeable moods during this period, undoubtedly a result of the pressures he faced as his health deteriorated. We kept things running as smoothly as possible when he was in his office, in the hospital and at home for long periods of time. Our main goal was to avoid the further erosion of morale. Over time, however, as a means of coping with the pressures we ourselves were feeling, we tried not to let Dr. Arth's illness affect us emotionally. We tried simply to keep the department afloat. When at last he retired just a few months prior to his death, we felt both relief and a sense of loss.

Healing and the Future

With the arrival of the new chairman, the staff hoped for better times, but we were also apprehensive and on edge. We knew that the changes that had begun with Dr. Arth's illness would increase under the new chairman. Although we hoped the result of the change would be positive, we really did not know what to expect. We prayed for transformation; a long chapter had ended, another one was beginning.

The new chairman had been a member of the museum's Education Department during the early 1970s, and was returning to the museum after 14 years to take over the department. He had continued a professional association with Dr. Arth and with many of the staff during that period. As a member of the Visiting Committee that had done the evaluation, the new chairman was very much aware of the stresses the Education Department staff were experiencing due to Dr. Arth's illness and the pending reforms that were expected.

The new chairman faced a situation in which old suffering and staff conflicts had to be resolved before major change could be implemented. The hierarchy-of-command organizational framework that was encouraged and jealously guarded by Dr. Arth had also been adopted, in part through default, by the program managers.

A policy of involving staff in the department's decision making process started with monthly meetings of the program managers and the full staff in which information updates on programs and museum-wide policies were presented by the new chairperson and managers. These meetings were a forum for any staff member to ask freely questions about departmental operations and communications problems, or to discuss other issues of mutual concern. Not all staff were comfortable with this process because it was so fundamentally different from what they were accustomed to.

Buckley and Perkins in "Managing the Complexity of Organizational Transformation" from *Transforming Work* (Miles River Press, 1984) describe the reluctance to become stakeholders in change: "For both the organization and individuals, the commitment stage is a time of being torn between the potential of the new direction and the security of the old. The tension between these two forces can cause an imbalance that creates internal disequilibrium and external strife. Moving forward and yet holding back, the individual experiences attachments to the past and fear of the unknown future."

The new chairperson had to address the staff's tug of war with the past and its fear of the future as he proceeded with a gradual transformation designed to improve the fundamental operation and leadership structure in the department. He received support and approval from the vice president for public programs and the museum's director to promote all current teaching staff to "senior museum instructors." He also filled several long vacant positions and gave overdue promotions to a number of managers and support staff, thereby creating new career paths. This phase of the organizational change was instituted early in his four-year tenure, providing stability in key support positions and preparing for the next round of change to come.

To complement the structural changes, many of the staff were assigned to participate in special museum-wide program planning committees. To do this effectively, adjustment in the teaching schedules of the senior museum instructors was required. This action in particular began to add to the self-esteem of some and foster a collaborative interest in and group ownership of the department's short-term goals.

Over the past two years, we have seen important progress in internal communications among the department managers, teachers and support staff. Improvements in office operations with the addition of a computer network, some staff training, the development of four new programs, increased staff and a new departmental operations budget have all helped us provide better services to clients and have allowed, too, for some significant individual and group healing.

Although there has been a notable transformation, we are at a crossroads in the healing and self-renewal process in the Education Department. Our singular goal in the coming months and years is to have a productive and self-supporting organization with a shared vision and purpose.

Dr. Arth was a talented educator who accomplished a great deal for the museum and the Education Department during his tenure. And yet, among the staff who served during his long illness, his legacy is clouded by the way in which he handled the final years of his chairmanship. His inability to share openly and honestly with his colleagues the facts of his illness ultimately made a traumatic situation even worse, both for his staff and very possibly for himself. His personal management style of being staunchly professional—yet, distant, private and at times controlling and rigidly hierarchical—had, as all styles must, some flaws. In this situation, those flaws were emphasized rather than mitigated.

One lesson that can be drawn from this situation, and which can be of use to the management of all institutions, is that some degree of flexibility in a manager's professional philosophy and practice is essential. No management strategy, however successful in the past, will be the perfect choice for every situation that arises. A style that does not allow for an effective response to change is almost certainly doomed to failure at some point. Dr. Arth's response in the last years of his life fostered traumatic feelings of anger and disappointment among the staff. Sadly, an opportunity for positive challenge, creation and growth was lost.

The Syndrome of the First Paid Director

Motown Historical Museum, Detroit

Rowena Stewart

The definition of the word "first" in its most positive sense carries with it the aura of status, success, winning and, in many cases, a rather subtly defined context of power. It also implies an inordinate amount of pressure and stress, for once an individual has been perceived to be "the first," most often she almost immediately has to make a transition to another phase or level of functioning. Somehow she must maintain not only the status quo of the circumstances that brought her to the position in the first place, but simultaneously, control the forces that have now been influenced by the very occasion of being first.

Nowhere is this cat's cradle of events and circumstances more evident than in the long, meandering and sometimes circuitous route trod by so many committed souls who have expended all their energy into either the creation or development of nonprofit agencies in general, nonprofit arts and cultural agencies in particular, and museums and/or historic and cultural centers specifically.

My comments for this chapter come from long experience. Years ago, I worked first as a volunteer and then moved on to being a staff member, and then a founder, and finally, became the first professional director for two major historical museums. Each of the institutions provided me with a rare museum experience and also with a great respect for the founders and the administrators who have taken on the challenge of building and developing a vision and shepherding a much-needed private institution into an equally much-needed and valuable public resource.

The syndrome of the volunteer founding director evolving into the first paid museum professional, and the impact of that evolution upon the institution, the staff and the community in which the institution resides, is a phenomenon that bears further examination and analysis. The importance of this transition is such that it can—and often does—influence the direction of the museum's growth. And while it is understood that all change takes time, and no evolution is an overnight event, the very real fact of the matter is that how the transition evolves can well determine the actual destiny of the institution. The syndrome of the volunteer founding director and the first paid professional museum director is an issue, then, that cannot be taken lightly.

In today's harsh economic reality, questions about the leadership of any organization, whether it is for-profit or nonprofit, present challenges that must not only be answered, but answered thoughtfully and creatively. The fiscal pool that has for years been a source of sustenance for nearly all areas of the private and public sector is drying up. In the ensuing scramble to survive, both for-profits and nonprofits are recognizing that they must take a long look at themselves, build upon what is effective and discard what simply does not work. To use the business vernacular of the day, organizations and even agencies within the government itself are being taught to re-engineer themselves to increase their chances of making it to the end of this century and beyond. And while most of this re-engineering has been directed at for-profit corporations and the U.S. government, logic, common sense and today's economics demand that nonprofits should do no less.

Ensuring the stability of an organization through the evolution of agency leadership is a major step in the direction of strengthening the organization. Understanding the factors that will aid in weathering that transition will make that process much easier for the directors, the staff, the board, the community and, of course, the institution.

At this juncture, it might well be wise to ask, Exactly who are these individuals who carry so much of the museum within themselves? Who are these committed believers who are, in many ways, both the museum as well as of the museum? They are the founding director, usually unpaid, and usually the keeper of the original vision, who was present at the "birth" of the organization. They are also the paid museum director, who often steps in to shape the institution and guide it to maturity and that state of existence that we commonly refer to as "institutionalization."

The challenge of ensuring that a volunteer museum organization ultimately is properly institutionalized really relies on three central and essential bodies or entities: first, the founder and the board of directors; second, the staff of the institution; and third, the community in which the institution resides. There is also another "community" to be recognized at this point comprised of those organizations of similar institutions (i.e., other museums and cultural centers or historical centers) and also the potential funding agencies that hopefully will provide financial resources for programming, staffing and the other very real operating needs of the museum.

A museum professional is traditionally considered to be a person who has been in the field for a number of years, acquiring professional skills and possibly also acquiring classroom training in museum studies and practices. A museum professional might be defined as a person who wishes to help the community (and, in a larger sense, mankind) by teaching about the cultural contributions that other individuals and often other cultures have made to society. These museum professionals may well operate in a benefactor or philanthropic mode since they are driven by a desire to give "something" back that translates into educating the community.

For the purpose of this chapter, I describe a museum professional as one who, through a series or sequence of learning experiences in museums, is prepared for and capable of answering questions and otherwise solving problems, or presenting information relative to the field of museums and museum studies. This sequence of learning experiences may range from a formal course of already formatted studies in the field to training programs, seminars and work in museums and historical centers.

Each of these individuals bears witness to the joy, pain and passion of seeing the institution emerge and struggle bravely toward what can only be described as a coexisting independence and type of tragic bondage—the former because it no longer is just an idea, but in fact, now physically exists; the latter because now that the idea has been liberated into an independent state of physical existence, in many ways it is now restricted by the rules of being regulated, the rules of being directed and the rules of its day-to-day administrative and financial struggles.

In so many ways, the founder being the organization itself and the first director being of the organization is a burden of tremendous magnitude, and both the volunteer founding director and the first paid museum professional are equally experienced in what this burden entails. For no matter how loved the institution, nor how treasured the vision, the fate of the museum usually rests upon these individuals. And it is this burden as well as this enormous love of the agency that can be the focal point of the trauma syndrome. For you can love something so much—you can treasure the vision to such an extent—that you cannot easily release it, not even to those who have the experience or training to take the vision to its next level and thus develop it.

A recent phenomenon during these waning years of the 20th century is the growth of museum education programs in colleges and universities. Today we are seeing most museum professionals entering the museum world with advanced degrees or at least several years of postsecondary training in the field. However, while the museum professional very well may have the benefit of years of training and/or education and even a high level of respect for the skills that are brought to the table, that individual can by no means expect to rest upon her laurels. The museum professional must understand that although the skills that she brings to the volunteer organization are respected by many other museum workers and professionals, there can be no assumption that the respect automatically travels into the facility with her. Most often, the burden of proof of the director's skill level will lie in each new job. With each new directorship, with the advent of each new challenge to build, to create and to develop, the first paid museum professional again will find herself having to prove her level of skill.

We have spoken peripherally of museums, but what precisely is this artifact that we have named a "museum"? There are some 10,000 museums in this country, all coming from different perspectives. Yet all are a source of information and education to their respective communities. The definition of a museum, according to both the American Association of Museums and *The American Heritage Dictionary*, is an institution for the acquisition, preservation, study and exhibition of works of artistic, historic or scientific value. The word museum, of course, derives from the muse of Greek mythology—any of the nine daughters of Mnemosyne and Zeus who each presided over a different art or science. However, as a museum director, I have always loved the word because of its other definitions and have always felt that the latter definitions more closely explained the roles played by so many museums. The definition is beautiful. They are really "a guiding spirit and a source of inspiration."

Museums also come into existence via a number of routes. But perhaps the most frequent or common path is through the collector who suddenly finds there is too much collection and simply too little space to store it. Indeed, it is my experience that many historical societies, centers, and museums have come into existence because of the interest a certain collector or group of collectors had for a specific area of knowledge and information and the need that they had to tell others of their journey—and document that story to pass on to their descendents. In years to come, the collection will form an image and a map—not only of the era itself but possibly also of the collector. However, no matter how one defines a museum, the single, linking thread in this tapestry of information is education. Collectors, founders, development directors all agree that in the final analysis, the raison d'être for collecting lies in education.

Besides the museum's volunteer founding and later first paid professional director, there are many other committed people who have invested a good deal of time, effort and sometimes money in a fledgling organization that has proven its benefit and worth many times to the community. Many of these people have been with the organization virtually since its inception, and some of these volunteers have occasionally even served as directors. At some critical point in time, however, they have come to accept that the organization has grown to the point where some type of mechanism must be instituted for controlled and documented development. The founder may feel simply that the existing staff can no longer handle the number of visitors, or she may have some foresight that the agency is evolving beyond what she can comfortably control. She may even admit that it is now time to hire a professional director, but she may not be able to easily understand or interpret what is perceived as the incoming force of power inherent in such a position. Staff insecurities abound. There may be perceptions that the original direction of the museum is no longer the driving energy, and that the bureaucracy of management has suddenly overshadowed and then overtaken the institution.

It is during these tender times that the incoming professional director makes critical decisions that will affect both the short- and long-term growth patterns of the museum. These decisions are made first in terms of the training and then the most cost-effective utilization of existing staff and boards. The first order of business should be the training of the board of directors.

It has been my experience that focused training for the board of directors is the most logical and effective way to continue to develop and, indeed, ensure institutional growth. Unfortunately, however, the individuals who sit on boards are often intimidated by any discussion of what will help strengthen them, and thereby help strengthen the institution. While many of the individuals have been active on for-profit and nonprofit boards, they unfortunately do not always see the need for further training.

Over the years I have worked with several museum boards and have been struck by how differently they interpret the political clout that is a byproduct of board membership. Many of our board members serve on traditional boards elsewhere in the community, but are unable to transfer that experience to the museum board to provide the clout—and the financing—that is needed to ensure the institutionalization of the museum. It seems that in the African-American community, the reality is that traditional boards use minority members as community relations representatives. Those organizations or corporations expect nothing but access to the community. The minority board members never experience the true network of power, and the result is that very little of the power that is needed is turned back into the community or to the museum.

What has become even clearer to me in recent years is that minority board members actually come to the table with very little economic power, although they often possess enormous political power. Still, these members are valuable to the museum, and it is here that the experiences of the first paid professional museum director initially come into play. It becomes the responsibility of the first paid professional director to make the connection between the resources represented in both the public and private sectors and somehow interweave those resources so that they blend splendidly with the internal political dynamics of the museum world.

Rising—or in some cases, actually looming—above all of this is the chair of the board. The relationship of the first professional museum director with the chair is characterized as perhaps the most difficult of all, and the sharing of power is traditionally the main issue. It is imperative that the director understand that while theoretically there can be a sharing of power, in reality there is only one chairman and only one director. These are dangerous but still navigable waters. Most important, the process of transferring power from the chair to the first professional paid director must be smooth, graceful and accomplished with as little trauma as possible.

In Alex Haley's *Roots*, the elders speak at length about a misunderstanding that has flared in the village. One incident had led to another and there seemed to be a full-scale feud brewing, with neither of the principals apparently considering compromise or retreat. One of the elders clearly identifies the problem: "You must never surround your enemy."

I don't recall this quote to imply that boards or chairs or staff should be perceived as the "enemy." In fact, the opposite is the case. As part of the very real community support that is the museum's foundation, staff, board and chairs should all be regarded as potential resources. The point that I am making with this quote is that without compromise, without a very real acceptance of the status, power and ownership that is represented in these principals of the organization, there will be an extremely long and difficult route for the first paid professional director to navigate.

Therefore, if the board chair seems to be having difficulty adjusting to changes in power, it becomes the responsibility of the professional director to help make the adjustment, and in doing so, renegotiate the positions of power as often as is needed. The cliché of "If at first you don't succeed, try, try again" is extremely real in the museum world. If the director is not successful in her negotiations at the outset, she should simply leave it alone and return to the issues at a later date. It should be noted here, however, that while experience shows that chairs very seldom change their position without justification, a good director will continue to negotiate until desired changes occur.

Indeed, one of the critical problems facing the first professional director is recognizing the staff and the volunteers who have been a part of the growth and the development of the fledgling organization. Staff as defined here may be paid or volunteer. The staff, which all along has been witnessing the transition and evolution of leadership and power, has also realized that with the advent of the new director will certainly come changes—both in personal leadership style and quite often in the character of programming. Under the old-style method of managing the transition, the staff would immediately feel the need to declare sides and loyalties. If they are themselves not trained but have simply been a loyal and steady presence for the many years they have worked alongside the outgoing founding director, there are inevitable feelings of anxiety and sometimes hostility toward the first museum professional. This anxiety and apprehension can also accompany a wave of unproductivity that is certainly not cost-effective to the agency. The first museum professional thus is faced with several immediate decisions.

After evaluating the staff to ascertain levels of competence, the director may decide to retain all or some of the staff. She may attempt to work with them and periodically provide them with needed training. This often occurs while the staff acts out its feelings of fear and insecurity, often by being uncooperative in subtle or not-so-subtle ways. Sabotage is certainly not unheard of in such situations.

The newly instated museum professional, of course, can opt to accept resignations from all staff. She may well feel that rather than attempting to maintain control over a staff that is both untrained and also seemingly loyal to the outgoing director, it would be easier on the institution to simply start anew with individuals selected by the incoming museum professional and director.

However, the resignation of the staff might well have an extremely negative impact on the local community that also must be wooed into either (1) continuing to support the agency as it comes under "new management," or (2) becoming an organized part of the institution's support base for the first time. Also, unless new staff members are waiting in the wings to take the place of the outgoing staff, there will be obvious and definite "holes" in the staff that would certainly not help develop a fully and effectively functioning office and agency. All of this prolongs the time required for the new museum professional to "come up to speed," and valuable time and momentum may be lost during the interim.

At any rate, it is imperative that if some or all of the staff are laid off, the community is informed of the rationale for this decision as soon as that process begins. While this does not lessen the pain of the layoffs for any of the parties involved (including the newly instated director), it does provide the beginnings of a degree of trust between the newly instated director and the community. My own experiences have run the gauntlet from having to request mass resignations from staff to understanding the traumatic impact staff unemployment can cause on a fragile community. I have in some cases negotiated with employees who have opted for training, and given those employees time to achieve their goals. Every first director must meet these types of challenges and make decisions based upon the options she sees. It is also wise to recognize that staff may either simply feel caught in the transition of leadership, or that there may be a very real danger connected with shifting loyalties, the perceptions of board members or even the perceptions of the chair.

Happily, most staff members are not hostile to the new director once she explains her positions. In most instances, the incoming director can become a major force in helping staff to make necessary adjustments, identify their individual potential roles in the new institution, and thus continue to grow with the institution.

New directors and institutions should understand that transition, evolution and voluntary relinquishing of power don't take place overnight. Often, at least a year will pass before any of these processes are completed. However, it is in completing those very processes that trust and faith in each other's abilities do develop. And it is in passing through this process that the mission of the organization—to educate and deliver information to the community—is also accomplished.

The community shares ownership with an organization that operates in its neighborhood. Therefore, a good relationship with the new director is absolutely critical. Relationships can be developed and maintained in many ways. I have designed public forums, shared expertise and experiences about the community with the community and acknowledged their contributions to the organization as well as to the community at large. If there is to be trust, it is imperative that the director have continued presence in the community.

Board support must be present at all levels, whether in programs, rituals or forms of festival and celebration and including all the classes or social strata of the community. Founders and volunteers will prove invaluable in helping to ease the transfer of power and the subtle transitions of leadership.

In the final analysis, it is the diverse characteristics of both the private and public sectors that merge in a single common denominator—funding. In the corporate world, it is the "bottom line" that drives the economic health of the company. With nonprofits, it is the ability to capture the essential and necessary capital from funding sources that drives the programming. How an institution is perceived to survive its leadership evolution or transition can determine how it continues to develop and be nurtured by the community—whether that community is the organization's actual physical site or whether, in a larger sense, the community is indeed the assembly of like organizations that compose the nonprofit organization's immediate family or associations.

In terms of continually communicating with the community, it is essential that radio, print media and, if possible, television contacts be established. All of the media must be involved and informed regarding programs and/or changes taking place within the museum. The media can thus provide reports to the community on the status of the evolving museum. No decision affecting the museum that may potentially have a major impact on the community should be made without residents being aware of the potential developments. Such events might include the firing or resignation of a principal or major employee of the museum, or the writing of a controversial bill regarding the museum's ultimate location. Whatever the event, if it is of major consequence to the organization and the community, the community should be informed. Once again, it is by so doing that trust develops in the director, the board and the museum itself. And it is because of this trust that the museum will continue to be successful in its collecting and archival programs; the community will feel that it is "safe" to entrust the valuable documentation of its time and lifestyles to the museum for preservation, for interpretation, for education and finally, ultimately, for communicating to generations not yet born that we were here, and that we wanted them to know the details of our journey.

Looking Back

Imagine being contacted by a head hunter who says a museum needs an executive director with your experience in the field. You are a professional with valuable contacts and a wealth of experience with fledgling institutions and numerous prior successes. The head hunter believes you would be perfect for this institution, which has been run by its founder up to this point. You would be the first professional to run this museum and you are lured by the challenge of making an institution out of a fledgling organization. Your ego tells you to go for it, and the head hunter assures you that this institution needs your expertise.

So you take the job. Within the first seven days you realize that all you have is a raw product that has operated on the energy of the founder and the founding board. You discover that nothing is really what it seemed. There is no money and there are no contacts. You now feel that you have made an enormous mistake. The questions become Where do I go from here, and How do I pull this off?

It is under these circumstances that two forces play on the same court: the dream of turning a nontraditional museum into a traditional museum, and the reality of such an undertaking. The truth is that reality always wins. As the first director, you face the challenge of creating an institution that meets traditional museum values, but you must also deal with a nontraditional community and audience. Nothing is what it seems to be. This is what I learned as the first paid director of such an institution.

Looking back on my initial reaction to this experience, I have assessed the situation and determined that there are several things I would have done differently. I would have done in-depth research on the organization much like any other project or grant. First I would have surveyed the funding world and spent time within the community to determine whether the institution is financially viable and whether the community considers it valuable. Community perception can influence an organization's ability to survive. My next step would have been to talk to all the board members and assess their understanding of their role, which greatly influences their relationship with the executive director and their ability to be effective. It is also important to find out if the board and founder are one and the same.

Researching the staff and how closely connected they are to the founding director is another key step I would have taken. The nature of this relationship can affect your ability to be effective within the institution and make the change you were hired to bring about. By speaking directly to the staff you can assess where the institution is professionally. The stress a staff experiences can be severe when the board and the executive director are not in sync. It is important that staff understand that the executive director is in charge and that they expect to be supported in their work and receive constructive feedback. You also gain an understanding of what is really going on within the institution and its culture.

If I had to do it all over again, I would have kept my ego in check and I would have been wary of the "syndrome of the first paid director." I would have negotiated a contract that included a therapist and specific time within the calendar year for rest and relaxation. I also would have taken an extended vacation somewhere warm and tropical to prepare myself for the task ahead. Having a mentor to help monitor my progress would have been imperative, since being too close to a situation can impair your ability to assess everything going on within the organization.

With all this in mind, I'd like to paint a different picture. Imagine being contacted by that same head hunter. He says that you would be the first professional to run this institution. The community is excited about the institution's continued progress and the founding board is eager to meet you. The funding community is already responding well to the institution's projects and purpose. There is an emerging mechanism for constant feedback with the community that you will be able to build upon and support. Although inexperienced, the staff are eager to learn and bursting with enthusiasm. The board understands its role and fiduciary duties and wants the executive director to have significant responsibility. The founding director is eager to assist in the transition and is prepared to take on a new role.

Your ego tells you to go for it, and the head hunter, founding director and board assure you that this institution needs your expertise. After discussing the pros and cons with your mentor, you are convinced you should take the position. So you take it. In negotiating your contract, you receive not only a therapist but several paid vacations each year so you can rejuvenate. Within the first seven days you are pleased to find numerous contacts, funding sources and community support. You are pleased you came to this institution. All the necessary elements are in place for successfully dealing with any challenge. You have made a wise decision and you are confident that you can pull this off. You are fully prepared to beat the syndrome of the first paid director. You can make a difference.

For the first paid director of an institution, the experience can be as problematic as the first scenario or as rosy as the second. What I have learned is that the professional always risks being blamed when things don't go as everyone had hoped. Preparing for the worst and maintaining your professional standards is wise. With any luck your fledgling organization will see your tenacity and commitment as an example to follow and decide to help you create a traditional museum.

You must ask yourself if it is all worthwhile and if it can work. I believe it can. The proof is the 10,000 museums around the country that have stood the test of time. The real challenge to all professionals is continuing to build bridges that are easier to cross.

Part Three

Governance

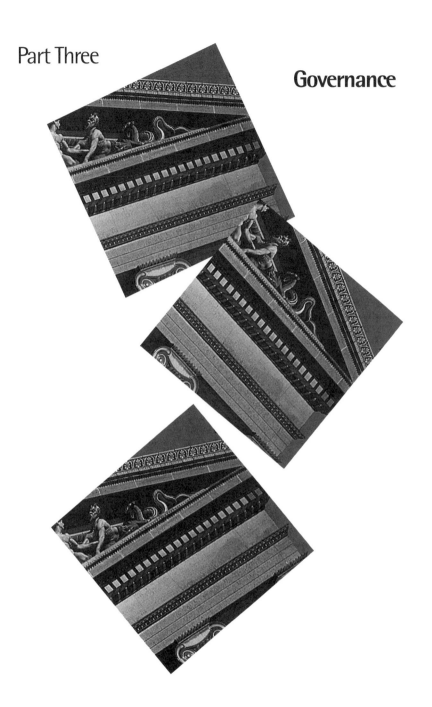

The Long March to the New Museum: A Work in Progress

The Kalamazoo Public Museum, Kalamazoo, Mich.

Patrick Norris

If once we are separated from our mother country, what new form of government shall we adopt, or where shall we find another Britain to supply the loss?
—James Dickinson, 1767

The Kalamazoo Public Museum's roots stretch back to the 1880s when its parent institution, the Kalamazoo Public Library, first began collecting artifacts and specimens. The Kalamazoo Museum was not founded until 1927 and it remained a department of the Kalamazoo Public Library through two locations and one name change until 1984, when for a short period it became a separate institution.

This period of titular independence turned out to be an interim in the museum's history, a transitional phase between a museum that could no longer prosper "as is, where is" and a museum that had not yet come to be. In this period, one board of trustees governed three separate entities: a $50-million school system, a $3-million library system and a $300,000 museum. The museum also shared the main library building, taking up one-third of its space. Conflicts of interest were inevitable and often public. Divestiture of both the library and the museum became the school superintendent's expressed desire, and a strategic objective that was achieved by the school board in 1990 and 1991, respectively.

The overarching question that occupied the minds of the museum staff and its friends in this interregnum was James Dickinson's question, first voiced in the literary debate that preceded American independence: "If once we are separated from our mother country, what new form of government shall we adopt, or where shall we find another Britain to supply the loss?"

This chapter will touch on events between 1984 and 1991 that provided an answer to that question. Our discussion focuses first on a series of changes through which one particular museum transformed its character and elevated its prospects. Along the way we will explore the quality of that experience: its impact on staff, stakeholders, and the director himself. Finally we will draw some lessons from the experience.

Our theme is modernizing a museum, finding new ways of doing things. This chapter is written by the director and from his dual perspective: both as an initiator of change, a source of institutional trauma; and as its victim, a staff member responding to events. We are all in this together and we are all in this alone.

The New Director

It is true that around every man a fatal circle is traced beyond which he cannot pass; but within the wide verge of that circle he is powerful and free; as it is with man, so it is with communities.
—Alexis de Tocqueville

In 1983, when it had become clear that the Kalamazoo Public Library and Museum (KPL&M) building was inadequate for the growing needs of two institutions, the school board appointed a Futures Committee to explore the space requirements and program needs of both. The committee's final report concluded that the museum needed to move out of the KPL&M building to free space for library needs and to finally gain its own identity.

It recommended further that the museum raise its image through aggressive programming and that it broaden its user base beyond the city school district to prepare for the campaign for a separate home. In 1984 the school board changed the museum from a library department into a separate institution. Soon thereafter, the director left for another museum.

When I became director of the Kalamazoo Public Museum in June 1985, a year had lapsed since independence. I was hired as the first museum director who, like the library director and school superintendent, reported directly to the school board. The museum was now officially one of three separate institutions. But its formal independence was limited by the realities of its size, and its significance was measured against the needs of a library system and a public school system.

I was also a new director in a personal, experiential sense. I had begun my career seven years earlier as director of a Bicentennial project that had become a start-up institution and I had spent the last five as a department head in a large urban museum. Managing a mid-sized museum, working with a staff of 10 civil servants and three public school unions, interfacing with public school and public library administrators, reporting to an elected board distracted by school and library concerns, discussing museum business in open board meetings and operating in the eye of press coverage were all new experiences for me. I realized a new game was afoot when my very first employment interview was held in front of microphones and before a live audience of my future employees and their library brethren. But at the beginning, I had little idea how it should be played.

My challenge was to revive the staff, redefine standards and reposition the public museum on the community agenda. The chief obstacles were less financial than programmatic and interpersonal. Although the museum was funded by a property tax, funding had to be renewed by a public vote at three-year intervals. We shared a library tax that had been renewed just before I arrived. While we lacked the authority to dictate change, we had the power to persuade. We had been told by community leaders what needed to be done: raise the image, broaden the base and bide your time.

Separation from the library meant just that: a former library department quickly had to become a viable entity, a museum in and of itself, at the same time that its performance had to persuade community leaders to invest in a separate facility. We had not been traumatized by a single event, but history had thrust us into a development process, a long trauma where stress was omnipresent: generated by a new director feeling his way, a board of elected amateurs wrestling with the needs of an urban school system, an inexperienced staff doing new things in new ways for uncertain prospects, and affecting us all was the very public environment in which we had to manage change.

I was given a three-year contract to turn around a business in trouble. I had inherited what is recognized in the management literature as "a fix-it." I had three years of tax funding with which to work. For the staff and for the director, the underlying challenge was survival. Could we emerge with our principles, our perspective and our sense of humor intact, despite the potential of what sports writers call "career-threatening injury?"

The Plan

There seems to be no plan because it is all plan. There seems to be no center because it is all center.
—C.S. Lewis

Between 1986 and 1991, because of four retirements, two new positions and two resignations, I was able to rebuild the staff. Together, with school board support and public involvement, we developed a new vision of the public museum premised upon two five-year goals: to refocus the museum as a human history museum and to earn accreditation by the American Association of Museums.

We recognized that the museum's external environment and its internal capabilities had changed since 1960 when the public museum moved into the new KPL&M building. An art center and nature center had grown up into thriving institutions. They were housed in newer facilities designed as museums. They had become identified with modern art and art instruction, and with regional ecology and agricultural history. They had specialized in particular modes of interpretation: registered courses and lectures, art exhibitions, nature camps, and living history.

We decided to do what the art center and nature center were not doing and what the public museum with new staff and direction was now able to do and do well:

• exhibitions of broad appeal in the humanities—specifically, history, technology and culture—designed to attract people who were not traditional museum visitors;

• interpretative programs that did not require tuition, registration or weekly time commitments;

• special events that offered families a way to spend time together, especially on weekends, and to improve the quality of time they might otherwise devote to visiting a mall or going to a movie.

The Futures Committee's recommendations framed this approach by setting three strategic objectives for the museum's planned renewal:

• operational integrity as a museum

Even with administrative separation from the library accomplished by board resolution in 1984, several years of restructured operations and remodeled expectations were needed to achieve a separate identity. AAM's Museum Assessment Program I (MAP I, 1986) helped prioritize our needs as a museum rather than a library department, and provided a checklist of changes that were needed to achieve AAM accreditation. MAP II (1987) set priorities for long overdue professionalization of the museum's collections management. By 1990 the museum was able to apply for AAM accreditation; in 1991 it was formally accredited.

• development of a new programmatic identity and image

In 1986 the museum commissioned a six-month marketing project that helped us redefine the museum's service as successfully expended quality time; its target audience as families in leisure times; its lead products as delivered through special exhibitions and varied interpretive programs; and its measure of success as visitation.

The popularity of one exhibit, "Dinosaurs Invade the Public Museum" (1986), persuaded the school board to approve conversion of 2,000 square feet of the library auditorium into a special exhibition gallery (1987) and to okay annual use of the full auditorium (4,600 square feet) for one large special exhibition. Successful grants and a separate 30 percent increase in tax revenue, which we won at the polls when the operating funding was renewed (1988), funded a makeover of the museum's long term exhibits and an upgrade of its planetarium (1988-91).

• relocation of the museum to a separate facility

The board of education appointed three additional citizen committees to prepare a strategic plan for a new facility (1988-1990). The underlying, if unstated, issue became apparent as these committees worked. In an era of declining public resources and increasing competition with the needs of the public schools, how would the museum secure the funds needed to operate, let alone build, any new museum?

Discussions with sources of foundation, corporate and individual support made it clear that any case for private capital support had to be premised on a continuing ability to operate a new larger museum. These potential donors expressed unwillingness to contribute to a single school district's entity, especially when the cost to operate a new facility would require voters in that single school district to triple the museum tax. Only by securing tax support from the museum's real users—the entire metropolitan area—could the museum generate an income adequate for running a new facility.

These realities led inescapably to the conclusion that a new museum would require a change in governance to a broader tax base. Given the challenge of the school board's primary role, its elected trustees were unable to commit to a capital campaign for the museum. They were also unwilling to issue bonds to build a new facility or raise taxes to operate it. If the public museum were to grow, it clearly would have to be spun off from the Kalamazoo School District to a larger local government unit.

In 1990 the school board secured the commitment of senior community leaders to explore how this might be done. The Museum Resource Group recommended a change in governance to the Kalamazoo Valley Community College district, a county-wide area encompassing 10 school districts. In April 1991, the community college formally assumed governance of the museum. But voters in the Community College District still had to approve the funding needed to operate it. In June they narrowly approved a new property tax for museum operations, extending the tax rate heretofore levied in only the Kalamazoo School District across an area encompassing 10 school districts. Voters agreed to a tax rate that will generate approximately $1.4 million a year, enough to operate a new 60,000-square-foot museum. Two months later, the Campaign for the New Museum was announced with $12.4 million pledged in lead gifts and a 24-month fund-raising timetable that has since been largely met. Over 90 percent of the funds needed to construct the facility had been pledged when ground was broken in September 1993. The new museum will open in 1996.

Some Lessons of Experience

I wake to sleep, and take my waking slow.
I find my fate in what I cannot fear.
I learn by going where I have to go.
—Theodore Roethke

Our institutional trauma was not the trauma of a sudden blow like the loss of funding or the firing of a director, although both were possible at different stages along the road.

Instead we experienced the cumulative trauma of a chronic condition with its good days and bad. All lived under the cloud of that ever-present question: What new form of government shall we adopt?

Having reached goals that the Kalamazoo Public Museum had pursued for a decade—AAM accreditation, two changes in governance, three successful tax referenda, program renewal and gallery renovation, and the start of a capital campaign—it is appropriate to count the costs as well as the successes of our institutional life between 1984 and 1991. Trauma scars those who live through it, but it also teaches. The trauma inherent in modernizing the way a museum operates inevitably changes the way a director does business. Traveling this far in the journey has left some lessons worth sharing. Here are four that I have learned by going where we had to go.

1. Turnarounds have their own life cycle and their own rhythms.

We moved from the period when the future of the museum was indefinite into the period when what was going to happen increasingly became a given. We passed through a middle interval when any successful outcome seemed in doubt. An entrepreneurial, aggressive style of public leadership and a coaching style of staff leadership (high on task and group maintenance behaviors) fit those years when we needed to establish the reality of independence from the library, reshape the museum and keep the issue of a new facility alive.

This style began to be a liability in the middle period when the board members who had separated the museum from the library and then hired me were replaced by members who were not party to this history and who saw a new museum as only the director's idea. In continuing to press for movement toward a new facility when no real progress was possible, I may have kept the hope alive, but at a personal cost. For a time, even raising the suggestion of new governance was viewed as a threat to new board leadership.

Eventually and to a large extent fortuitously, the idea of a new museum moved to the top of the community agenda. Factors beyond the school board's control and my own brought into the picture stakeholders with the influence and resources to undertake the project. The museum project began to be viewed as an integral component in downtown redevelopment and as a good fit with the community college. When our future was attached to the interest of these community enterprises, we learned a new lesson about the importance of museum (and museum staff) in the greater scheme of things: that we were one of many good civic projects and lucky indeed to have our turn at bat.

The school superintendent, not the museum director, represented the school board on the Museum Resource Group where basic decisions shaping the museum's future were reviewed. Once the issue rose to the top of the community agenda, the institution passed into a phase when strangers—local corporate leaders and foundation executives—were closer to its fate than the director and staff. This was a painful reality for us all, and we did not emerge unscathed. For the director, it was a season of low-status leadership. For some members of the staff, a period of disillusionment ensued.

2. Leadership and followership are situational.
Different times demand different styles of leadership, and of followership. As the ground of our institutional being shifted, we were forced to shift our assumptions with it. Both have shifted at least twice already, and we are due for more change. The challenge of turning around a museum in 1985 differed from the challenges of accepting outside leadership in 1990 and the challenges of enlarging the scope of the institution in 1993. Central emphases of a turn-around situation were building a new culture and developing a team—group maintenance behaviors. Today, task behaviors—simply getting a job done on time and under budget—frequently outweigh group maintenance needs.

As a staff we have had to learn that not all decisions can or ought to be made by consensus. We have also learned that we do not always participate in the decisions that shape our destiny. The rituals of team building—the group field trips and all-nighters before exhibit openings—are still central to building trust in the good intentions of director and key staff, if not unquestioning faith in their wisdom.

3. Tolerance for ambiguity varies with personality and proximity to the heat in the kitchen.
In the course of speaking to, negotiating with and, above all, just listening to other voices, the director acquires an appreciation of the museum as one of many worthy institutions in the community. She also gains an appreciation of complex situations in all their hues: charcoal gray, banker's gray, blue gray and silver gray. This acceptance of ambiguity is both an occupational necessity and a survival skill, the natural result of becoming acclimated to the heat in the kitchen.

Because staff members tend to be sheltered by position and normal responsibility from daily contact with the same externalities, they tend to see issues in starker tones, more black and white and less gray. In taking ownership of an institution, they take justifiable pride in their own achievements. Indeed, as professionals, they probably understand them better than stakeholders. Ownership can blind as well as build a staff.

4. Good people leave; good people stay on.
The director lives at the center of battle, responsible for starting it and at the same time, one of its victims. The director is positioned at the neck of an hour glass. The sands come alternately from above and below, and seldom do circumstances allow the glass to rest.

The director lacks the freedom to indulge emotions and expressions that staff, board and community members exercise and enjoy.

As a coping strategy, directors develop a game face to wear for the world and a connotatively neutral vocabulary to speak to it. But learning to "depersonalize" language and "objectify" personally painful situations is an acquired skill, one that, like applying makeup, takes time to do well and looks awkward until it is mastered.

When the ground shifts beneath an institution, cracks begin to appear in the solidarity of a staff. Any fundamental change can threaten some members of the staff and some friends of the institution. They begin to lodge expectations that the director may be unable at the moment to fulfill. They engage in organizational and community politics to affect situations that they do not understand and cannot control. A sense of ownership can become an illusion of mastery when new stakeholders exercise a legitimate interest in the community's museum. In these moments, we learn the cost of stewardship: the museum really does belong to the community, not to the staff. Some staff members adjust to a loss of mastery, but others cannot. Because the museum is no longer the institution that they knew or built, times of trauma are finally the times when good people part company.

Conclusion

Ambiguity is the warp of life, not something to be eliminated. Learning to savor the vertigo of doing without answers or making shift and making do with fragmentary ones opens up the pleasures of recognizing and playing with pattern, finding coherence within complexity, sharing within multiplicity.
—Mary Catherine Bateson, 1994

Today, four years after the events described in this chapter, we remain in a process of change, adaptation and improvisation. The merger of the public museum into the community college has carried the museum staff into a new corporate culture, introduced a new set of internal stakeholders and added further refinements to the way we do business. At the same time, the complex undertaking of building a new museum and cooperatively creating a new vision of what the museum could become has helped us begin to understand, embrace and implement the ideas of new stakeholders whose labor made the project possible. Although we are still on the road, the destination is in sight. The new facility is scheduled to open in the spring of 1996.

If there is any final lesson to be drawn from the journey so far, it may be this: ambiguity, uncertainty and partial answers, as Mary Catherine Bateson reminds us, are normal ever-present conditions of an organization reinventing itself. Changing scope—including new stakeholders, adopting different modes of operation, co-creating a new museum—

has forced us to discover common meanings and shared visions in order to survive, both individually and institutionally. Perhaps in learning the lessons of changing our institutions, we may begin to understand the patterns of changing ourselves and, ultimately, our country. I hope so.

Life on a Fiscal Precipice

The New-York Historical Society

Holly Hotchner

On February 3, 1993, the board of trustees of the New-York Historical Society (N-YHS) voted to close the institution, which was on the brink of bankruptcy. In January of that year, galleries had been closed and staff cut. Now the library and research services were closed, public programs canceled and the remaining staff of 75 reduced to a skeleton staff of 35 people. *The New York Times* heralded the event with the headline "A SOCIETY BECOMES HISTORY" and commented: "After 188 years, with a crowd of 120 gathered outside, the N-YHS closed its doors. Will it ever reopen? Stay tuned." The next day the *Times* asked: "IS THIS THE END FOR NEW YORK'S ATTIC?" Between October 1992 and April 1993 literally hundreds of articles were generated nationally and internationally about the fate of New York's oldest museum and one of America's finest research libraries. The month the institution was closed, an advisory committee was assembled comprised of board members, three senior staff members including myself, and outside advisors. We were to complete the herculean task, within four weeks, of coming up with a rescue plan that could be immediately implemented not only to bring in funds to the cash-starved Society, but more importantly to map a future for general operating support. There had been many other cash crises and cash bail-outs in the institution's history. Other advisory groups had been assembled, the institution had been restructured and five new administrations put in place over a nine-year period. But miraculously the institution had never actually been forced to close.

During my 11 years at the Society I was the only senior manager to serve under five CEOs, all of the restructurings, the changes of board chairs, presidents and directors, and was also the only one to weather both near-bankruptcies. In this chapter I will discuss the events leading to the closing of the N-YHS and the plan that grew out of this crisis. I will focus on public perception, as created by the press, and specifically the media's effect on the staff. The numerous crises I will touch on are: severe financial crisis, change of mission and purpose, leadership, change of directors and CEOs and attempted mergers with other institutions. All of these occurred in an environment of extreme negative public perception, and almost all were out of the staff's control.

For many people, it was only when the Society was in crisis that it entered their minds. The institution was nicknamed the New-York Hysterical Society for the seemingly never-ending series of crises that continually rocked the institution. There were widespread opinions about how the Society got to where it was and what should be its ultimate fate. Finger-pointing and blaming were rampant—from the press at large, public officials, members of other nonprofits and the general public. A declining reputation and lack of credibility as an institution (a problem that had existed for years) had a long-range debilitating effect on the staff. The numerous attempts at new starts ultimately could not overcome the lack of a large endowment, an influential and energetic board and a clearly defined and marketable sense of purpose.

Background

As early as 1825, then only 20 years old, the institution faced its first fiscal crisis. Its existence was threatened by a seemingly insurmountable debt of $7,500. Its doors were closed for nine months while a sale of part of the collection to ensure survival was contemplated. At the last moment, through a generous act of the state legislature, a grant of $5,000 saved the Society from dissolution. Ironically, this set of events precisely foretold the institution's future 168 years later.

Many other economic problems had hounded the institution. In 1872 the cash-poor institution was unable to raise the money to build on the Fifth Avenue site between 79th and 85th streets and relinquished that land to the newly formed Metropolitan Museum of Art. In the 1970s and early 1980s a series of sales from the collection took place to bring in urgently needed funds.

A New Era

In 1982, James B. Bell, the new director, inherited 184 years of poor management decisions and an institution that was isolated from New York's cultural community. Bell stated in the press, "We've lived a club-like existence and we're not going to do that anymore." The institution had long been criticized for operating as an elitist club failing to reach out to the public or to elicit public funds. As London's *Art Newspaper* put it in March of 1993: "During the 60s, 70s, 80s, when other institutions realized that there was no way that they could build up an endowment without catering to the masses, and without appealing to the federal government, museums went cap-in-hand. The N-YHS could not bring itself to do that. It was run like a club. It closed its eyes to what was going on." "The Society functioned as a laid-back yet scholarly private club," commented the publication *The New York Observer*. "A seat on the Board of Trustees was an inherited post for the descendants of old New York families." Board meetings had been conducted in Dutch for much of the institution's early history.

I was hired by James Bell in 1984 as chief conservator to create a comprehensive conservation and preservation plan for the Society. In the 180 years of the institution's history there had been no systematic overview taken of the collections or a program created for their care. Although relatively little was known about the museum collections at large, there were three published catalogues of the paintings collections. I was one of a few in the scholarly community who suspected that there were many unknown treasures in

"New York's attic." However, no one, myself included, was prepared for the astonishing scope of this task. By 1988, when an inventory had been completed, it was estimated that the museum collection was comprised of nearly 1 million objects!

I was intrigued by the changing attitude of the board of trustees and by the opportunity to be a part of turning the institution around. Although unaware at the time of what this would entail, I was attracted by the challenge of professionalizing the care, management and interpretation of such a nationally important collection.

The goals for the staff were generated as the collections became known. I was able to convince the board that the first step in any collections management and/or deaccessioning program had to be knowing what we had, where it was, what condition it was in, and how it related to the overall collections. As chief conservator, over the next four years I planned, raised funds for and implemented three conservation labs and hired a professional staff of conservators and technicians. Together we devised a 30-year preservation program. Under my direction, this new, highly dedicated staff of conservators and registrars salvaged the collections and moved them into improved storage facilities. In addition, a comprehensive conservation program and physical inventory was undertaken.

There was a great deal of staff pride about what had been accomplished in a short period of time. One of my personal goals was to create a team of professional curators, conservators and registrars who could work as equals for a common goal—something which, I had found, did not always exist in other museums.

The 1988 Crisis

Unfortunately, major funds were not raised between 1984 and 1988. By 1988 the endowment had dwindled, the budget deficit had mounted and the capital problems had reached a new urgency as the roof began to leak. In order to bring in urgently needed income, the board had contemplated selling further portions of the collections (this action was stopped by the New York State attorney general) and proposed building a 33-story tower over the building itself (a measure that was to be loudly protested by the community and the landmarks commission and did not go forward).

In June of 1988, the institution received national attention as it was driven to the brink of financial disaster. Two floors of the institution were closed and one quarter of the 106-member staff was suddenly dismissed. Along with the rest of the staff, I was given no prior warning of this event. To make matters worse, that August the previously poor state of the storage of the paintings collection was revealed to the public on the front page of *The New York Times*. This article brought the matter to the attention of the state attorney general as well as the public.

Although the vast majority of the public had no prior perception of the N-YHS, the institution now became widely thought of as "that place with moldy and deteriorating paintings." It was not known that a highly dedicated staff of conservators and registrars had been working since 1984 to rectify the overall conditions. Six months prior to the *Times* article, the staff had moved the collections into new museum-standard storage facilities. A comprehensive conservation program had been underway since 1986, as had a physical inventory of the objects. Although the staff had already worked diligently to rescue the collections, the objects had become stigmatized by the media as "ruined." The staff was encouraged that the urgency of the general economic decline was heeded, but their work over the past four years was not being acknowledged. Furthermore, as a senior manager, I had not been able to predict the actions of the board or the press. This led to general discouragement and disillusionment. By the fall of 1988, Bell and his deputy director had resigned.

Another New Era

The Society had apparently weathered the extreme fiscal crisis and appeared to be on the brink of a new era. The board of trustees modernized and augmented its bylaws. The total number of board seats was expanded to 50 and life-term seats for board members were abandoned in favor of a more modern system of board evaluation and term rotation.

Norman Pearlstine, at the time managing editor of *The Wall Street Journal*, had assumed the newly created position of board chairman. Barbara Knowles Debs, a former board member of the N-YHS and former president of Manhattanville College, agreed to become president and CEO (previously the board chair was the chief executive officer) in an interim period, and several new and powerful trustees joined the board. Debs restructured the institution into four operating units and significantly, in recognition of the great strengths of the three-dimensional and fine arts holdings, conferred equal status on the museum and the library.

As with many historical societies, the institution had always had at its core its extraordinary library, as it does to this day. The earliest collections were library and archival materials, and historically the librarian had been the director of the Society. However, unlike other historical societies, in its early years major collections of fine arts and material culture also came into the institution, largely because it was the only New York museum that could accommodate such objects. It had long been acknowledged that the great strength of the New-York Historical Society was the interrelatedness of the museum and library collections. However, the collections remained isolated from one another. To this day, their integration remains the greatest challenge.

As part of the restructuring, I was promoted into a newly created position of director of the museum. I was to organize and professionalize the management of the Society's collections of fine arts and visual and three-dimensional objects, and to develop a plan for their interpretation. When I became director, the museum staff was comprised of one registrar, one curator, one photo clerk and two technicians. Clearly, the staff had to grow dramatically in order to professionalize. Unfortunately, as we were to find out, the library, museum and external affairs (including education) units were set up without the ability to dramatically increase the overall budget. This created an internal tension between these areas as they competed for funds.

Change of any kind is often difficult, and I, in the newly created director position, was the initiator of change. However, the museum staff and I were unprepared for the understandable misgivings that the library staff had about the creation of the museum. From their point of view, the museum was created at the library's expense. The library staff had worked at the institution longest and maintained the institution's memory and history, whereas the newer museum staff came from various backgrounds with diverse expectations. Because Barbara Debs had a degree in art history, people assumed she favored the museum. Furthermore, we were constantly confronted by the ultimate question: How do you integrate a library and a museum when the technology is not quite there, there is no funding to do so and when practices in both professions are so different?

This basic schism, due in part to the very nature and function of museums and libraries, had existed throughout all periods of the institution's existence. It was translated into a dialectic between history and art, and research and aesthetics. The institution had to both maintain costly research services and attract a new, large audience. Despite the general respect that all the museum and library staff had for one another, "them" and "us" camps were created.

The First Advisory Board: 1989

At this time a distinguished advisory board was created to assist the Society in addressing its problems and to recommend a plan on fiscal and programmatic issues. The 12-member board included New York City officials and professionals from libraries, museums and financial institutions. Although some staff were consulted in this process, the board submitted an independent report. In the wake of financial crisis and with little economic base to build upon, all options were considered, including extinction, mergers with other institutions and significant reorganization.

The result of this process was a unilateral agreement that the Society should continue to exist independently as both a museum and library of American history and art. The mission of the Society was studied and revised to aid in the refinement of the collections and to direct the relationship of programs to resources. Financial recommendations included initiating an endowment campaign to raise $25 million by 1995, balancing the budget for three years in order to develop institutional credibility, and raising operating support from city, state and federal funds.

In many aspects, what Barbara Debs and Norman Pearlstine inherited was a 185-year history of poor management and a severe fiscal crisis. Their achievements over the next several years were many. Twenty-three million dollars were raised. Conservation, cataloguing and physical and intellectual access to the collections were made institutional priorities. Exhibitions and programs were developed to bring new constituencies into the previously isolated Society.

I was charged with the task of setting ambitious goals for the museum staff. They had to carry out, within months, what other institutions usually have many years to accomplish. Within the museum, thousands of objects had not been assessed or even examined in the light of day, much less properly catalogued. Storerooms were hopelessly overcrowded. There was no work space, much less staff or technical assistance to accomplish the work. Although I was permitted to increase staff, there was nowhere to put them. The offices, designed for a 10-person administrative staff in 1904, were woefully inadequate. I was also unprepared for the difficulties of recruiting a staff for an institution in such shaky financial condition.

Furthermore, the remaining staff were traumatized by years of crisis and budget cuts, as well as by expectations that did not match institutional resources. Little communication had existed among the administration, the museum and the library, and virtually none between the board and the staff. Consultants and advisors had repeatedly conducted institutional studies at compensation far exceeding that of the staff salaries. The reports involved the staff, but the recommendations and conclusions were rarely shared with them. Significantly, it seemed as if these reports had little effect. On top of all this, staff layoffs had come without warning. Despite any amount of hard work, the bottom line was repeatedly the lack of recurring operating funds.

AAM Reaccreditation

Part of my charge when hired was to lead the institution, with the president, through the AAM reaccreditation process, which had been postponed over the previous 12 years. Collections management policies were created, including accessioning and deaccessioning policies, and security and emergency procedures were established. An extensive loan and exhibition program was developed. When I arrived in 1984, the permanent collections installations had indeed been permanent—many had been in place since the 1950s. We discovered that it was much easier to take these installations apart than to install the kind of exhibitions that the staff were interested in, given that there was no specific exhibition or reinstallation funding, little staff and no lead time. Furthermore, it was difficult to attract loan exhibitions, given the lack of museum-standard climate control in the galleries. Under these circumstances, keeping the large galleries filled with interesting exhibitions and a new and large public became something of an albatross and weighed heavily on the staff.

Nonetheless, an ambitious exhibition and loan program was achieved and a coherent museum publication program initiated. This initiative culminated in a traveling exhibition of the original watercolors of John James Audubon, which opened at the National Gallery of Art and will continue through 1996. The exhibition was the first to be carried out with something approaching adequate funding and lead time. It has served to help the collections and institution gain deserved national recognition and has brought in about $1 million in earned income (including the books and related products), which virtually kept the institution open for a period of one year. In addition, under my direction the project was developed so that a good portion of the income went directly into the conservation and preservation of the Audubon collection. The entire collection was conserved, rematted and framed, and a new storage facility created with proceeds from the exhibition.

During the period 1984-1992, three conservation labs were installed, conservators hired for the first time and a 15- to 30-year preservation plan developed. We raised about $8 million directly for the collections, so that the paintings, drawings, prints, photographs, architecture, sculpture and decorative arts could be surveyed, inventoried and put on-line.

Another step forward was taken when an architecture department was established and its first curator hired. Known as a major repository for 19th- and early 20th-century architectural materials, the Society's collections had existed in limbo between the museum and library and received little attention. A model funding initiative was set in place. With leadership from a prominent foundation, federal, corporate and private sponsorship followed. We set out to study existing management systems for architectural collections and recognized that the task was overwhelming. For example, we found that the Mies van der Rohe archives at the Museum of Modern Art, with some 12,000 objects, had a staff of at least four people who had been cataloguing for well over six years. By comparison, the Society's architectural collections were estimated to be around 500,000 objects! Undaunted, the curator, conservator and a staff of one or two technical assistants rolled up their sleeves. Architectural collections were inventoried and cataloguing initiated for the first time in the Society's history.

A model state-of-the-art off-site study storage center was created for paintings, sculpture and decorative arts and all collections consolidated there for evaluation, study and refinement. A master plan for the physical plant was carried out and innovative public programs developed by the new department of public programs to reach a more diverse audience. For example, highly successful was the three-year program entitled "Why History?" The program brought new audiences and also offered programs that were tied to the institution at large and involved both the museum and library.

By September 1992, the entire process of AAM reaccreditation was prepared and the site visit accomplished. I include here excerpts from the accreditation Committee On-Site Report, from September 1992, which I believe was a very fair summary of the institution's plight:

> "The New-York Historical Society has seen and continues to face difficult financial times. Publicly criticized for alleged mistreatment of collections and suffering the loss of confidence that bad press causes, the Society faced the scrutiny and subsequent requirements of the New York State Attorney General. This attention to the Society has galvanized the institution's lay and professional leadership, causing intense focus on the documentation, storage, and care of collections and a very high awareness of the need for fiscal responsibility. . . . The New York Historical Society's staff is extremely competent, and the visiting committee was very impressed by its concern, grace under severe financial pressures, and clear commitment to the needs and causes of the institution. Their loyalty is unquestionable and admirable, and all of us wished that the future seemed both brighter and clearer for the Society. . . . At the same time, however, the Society's financial situation has not improved and may be worsening. The endowment remains at less than $10 million, expenditures remain relatively high; and no large, new sources of funds are assured or even reasonably in sight. This, along with the 1 October 1992 retirement of President Barbara Debs, calls into question the New-York Historical Society's ability to fulfill its mission and remain a viable organization."

In the end, due to the closure of the institution, accreditation was withdrawn.

Staff Morale

Given that staff achievements apparently could not combat negative public perception or make a dent in the overall fiscal problems, I tried to set up within the museum a system of creating short-term goals and celebrating them as they were achieved. Although gaining control of the collections was the stated institutional priority, each member of the greatly reduced staff had an overwhelming and somewhat unreasonable number of other responsibilities as well. Each curator, registrar, conservator and administrator was expected to plan exhibitions, programs, publications and capital projects and operate research collections.

Within this environment, tangible goals achieved and lauded with appropriate praise went a long way toward raising spirits. For example, when the cataloguing of the "A" buildings of the Cass Gilbert collection (numbering some 3,000 objects) was accomplished with an innovative program of students and volunteers assisting staff, a party was held with participants bringing foods beginning with that letter of the alphabet, like apples, avocados, etc. Although it may sound frivolous in the retelling, celebrating tangible milestones went a long way toward developing staff morale and rapport.

Too Little, Too Late

Despite great strides in fund raising, the $22 million raised was largely for programs, exhibitions, educational programs and specific collections projects, and did not significantly add to the endowment. Between 1988 and January 1993, the value of the Society's endowment dropped 27 percent and administrative costs increased to 40 percent of the operating budget. We learned the lesson that programmatic funding, although giving budget relief, often increased the operating budget and put more strain on an already overworked staff. The Society continued to operate at a deficit of around $2 million per year and the endowment continued to dwindle. All feasibility studies adamantly stated that the Society did not have the donor base to conduct a capital or endowment campaign and that general operating support had to be in place to attract endowment funding.

Innovative collaborations were tested. Cohabitation with The Jewish Museum took place for an 18-month period while construction of the new Jewish Museum building was carried out. This experiment, which I believe is one of the first models of a museum-within-a-museum, could serve as subject matter for an entire book. From an administrative point of view, it turned out to be a greater challenge than anticipated, and because the collaboration involved primarily exhibition spaces and therefore the museum, it served to further divide the museum from the library. Happily, programs and attendance increased. However, the collaboration did not serve to build lasting new constituencies of return visitors the Society had hoped to capture.

Mergers with other institutions were pursued to explore long-range viability for the Society. In the fall of 1991, discussions were held about merging with the Museum of the City of New York. Long considered advantageous from a collections and programmatic point of view, the merger had been proposed in the 1930s by Mayor Fiorello LaGuardia and had been urged in 1991 by New York City Cultural Commissioner Mary Schmidt Campbell. The discussions were held at the board level and both institutions were vulnerable to criticism if information leaks were to reach the press. It was recognized that the merger would save administrative costs and create a world-class history museum and research library. However, in the end the merger was not deemed viable at that time. Among other reasons, it was determined that it would take a one-time cash infusion to merge the two institutions, and these funds were not available.

I attended the Museum Management Institute during that summer and we often used the Historical Society as an extreme case study for fiscal, collections and legal issues. When I returned, the fiscal realities had deteriorated and any possibility of using my newly acquired skills in team management were remote. We were to learn the hard way that we could not govern by consensus. By October 1992, Barbara Debs had completed her term as president and Norman Pearlstine assumed the role of interim CEO. The remaining three senior staff members (me, the director of the library and the vice president for external affairs) were informed that there was not enough cash to remain open through January of 1993. This information was shocking even to senior staff. Cash flow was a continuous problem but the institution had always been able to make ends meet. It seemed inconceivable that after all the work and achievement relative to where we had started, the institution was once again on the brink of bankruptcy, just as it had been four years earlier.

Norman Pearlstine told *The New York Observer*, "The deficit never went away. At any given time, Irv the liquidator could have come in and said, 'You guys are out of business.' We were all aware of that . . . It was always the feeling that these were chances worth taking." Juliana Sciolla, chief operating officer for a number of months under Pearlstine, concluded that the institution's expenditures had increased in order to carry out extensive work to revitalize the ailing institution. "We had a decision to make—either close down or make a run for it," she said to *Manhattan Spirit*. "We had to demonstrate that we could turn the Society into a vital public institution. We knew we might not make it." Although the staff remarkably had achieved what it set out to do, apparently the institution would not make it.

Effect on the Staff of the Newest Crisis

The following six months were a perilous roller-coaster ride. The situation shifted from day to day. Rumors were abundant and the press began extensive coverage. Quite often, the staff and in some instances management and board, would all learn in the morning papers (accurately or otherwise) about plans and events. At what point should the entire staff be involved? Given how quickly things changed, what was there to say that would not deepen anxiety and lower morale?

Among the staff, there was initially a sense of anger that management had not anticipated this financial collapse. Despite all of their efforts and accomplishments, without long-term leadership and resources in place, the staff was to experience public blame and humiliation while being asked to work even harder. In the ensuing months the institution was relentlessly criticized, which could not help but reflect on the staff.

As the N-YHS again faced bankruptcy and possible dissolution, many staff members even questioned whether the Society should survive in its present state. As the employees worried about survival of their own positions, any remaining solidarity in the staff cracked, and the senior managers became the buffer zone for their anger.

The New York Public Library Proposed Loan and Merger

The Society needed an immediate cash infusion to buy time even to close in an orderly fashion. The CEO and financial officer informed us that with a $1.5 million loan the institution could remain open through June of 1993, but this amount would not ensure a future beyond June. Commercial banks refused loan money to an institution that had no source of income for repaying loans. Initially the New York Public Library (NYPL) was approached as a potential lender, while a possible merger between the two institutions was also under discussion. *The New York Times* headline read: "TO BE RESCUED HISTORICAL SOCIETY MAY END UP JOINING ITS SAVIOR." As with the possible merger with the Museum of the City of New York, the merger discussions were conducted by board members, to the exclusion of staff. In the absence of hard facts, rumors built relentlessly and the institution became even further polarized. Should the library be "taken over" to save the institution at large, and what did "takeover" imply? For a variety of reasons and despite all good will, neither the loan nor the merger came to pass.

Closing the Galleries

Unable to find a temporary "white knight," the Society closed its galleries on January 4, 1993. I was forced to lay off 15 staff members. This was a low point for me professionally, as I had hired most of these dedicated professionals and had convinced them to come work for the troubled institution. Despite my best efforts, in the end I had little input into this decision and my credibility was undermined. The final exhibition, "Restored Visions," which displayed 50 recently restored paintings, had been designed, in part, to herald the Society's recovery from the fiscal crisis and mismanagement scandal of four years earlier. To the staff, it symbolized much progress, but ironically marked the closing of the galleries and loss of the very staff who had made this progress possible.

The Sotheby's Loan

In December, the possibility was raised of borrowing the needed $1.5 million from Sotheby's. As with the Public Library discussions, the loan would have to be collateralized by objects from the collections. I had been instrumental in convincing the board to invest in the management of the collections and now the staff was under the gun to deaccession.

Although the staff had been at work over the previous two years in identifying objects appropriate for deaccessioning, and even though collateral objects would not necessarily be sold, there was now an imminent deadline to make hard and fast decisions. The task of coming up with $3 million worth of items from the collections (the loan had to be collateralized two-to-one) went on day and night over a two-week period. Stress and tension were at an all-time high.

Faced with possible dissolution of collections, loss of jobs and the imminent closing of the institution, the staff was diligent in trying to avoid ethical compromise in choosing the items to be offered as collateral. Ethics was one area in which each individual could exert control. The mood was grim at the staff holiday party held in January. There was little to celebrate. The senior managers were locked in conference to determine if the loan could go forward, thereby giving the institution a reprieve. When the loan agreement was announced on January 28, 1993, the staff breathed a collective sigh of relief. We believed that at least we had bought time until June.

It Can Always Get Worse

The ensuing course of events proved to be even more debilitating. Other cultural institutions and the press attacked the Society for the Sotheby's loan. Headlines in *The New York Times* read: "THE HISTORICAL SOCIETY IS CRITICIZED FOR USING ARTWORKS AS COLLATERAL." Several museum professionals went on record about the inappropriateness of this loan, declaring that the N-YHS had jeopardized its soul, and emphasizing that collections must never be regarded as liquid assets. Others expressed sympathy for the staff of the Society, pointing out that most museum professionals do not have the financial sophistication to cope with impending bankruptcy, and implied that it would be best for some troubled institutions to terminate themselves rather than allow others to handle the disposition of their collections. The staff knew how much effort had gone into making very difficult decisions precisely so that the collections would not be dispersed. *The New York Times* said the atmosphere at the Society was "as somber as its classical limestone facade." Instead of viewing the loan as an extraordinary gesture of good will, it was cast in a macabre light. In an April 1993 article in *Newsday*, this opinion was eloquently stated: "You need a board that does not heave a sigh of relief when the auction house Sotheby's offers a $1.5 million loan in return for $3 million in collateral. . . . Every politician knows that the appearance of wrongdoing is nearly as pernicious as the act itself—and to go to an auction house for a loan looks naive at best."

The staff, reeling and unprepared for this newest round of criticism, was to receive an even greater blow when it was announced days later that the loan would not, in fact, be used to keep the institution open until June. Norman Pearlstine was quoted in *The New*

York Times as saying, "We decided not to spend money on what won't get us where we want to go." On February 3, 1993, the board voted to close the institution and lay off more than half of the remaining staff. The three senior managers were given a matter of days to make the painful decision of which staff would remain. I found that even in a personal meeting with each of my 35 staff members—those who would be staying as well as those who would have to be let go—I could offer little explanation or comfort to those who felt duped or humiliated. Nor could I take any consolation in the progress that had been made. The decisions I had to make often were based on remaining funding and necessary areas of physical protection or stewardship rather than solely on merit or seniority.

The Advisory Committee, March 1993

A new advisory committee was assembled to determine what, if anything, could be done in this dire situation. The new committee had, on the face of it, tasks that were not dissimilar to those facing the advisory committee four years earlier. The primary distinction was that at this point the Society was completely out of time and operating funds. The committee was comprised of board members, outside advisors and three senior staff managers, including myself.

All options, some very drastic, were considered, including closing completely, liquidation of the collections, operating as a library alone, as a museum alone or merging with one or more institutions. This time we actually calculated the financial implications of closing and operating as a museum or library alone, not as an exercise but as possible realities. Since the last crisis we had known that operating the physical plant was a large expense in itself. I was given the task of coming up with the "dark" budget, as it came to be known. Although I did discuss aspects of this budget with various staff members, the implications of the task made it quite solitary. The resulting numbers were shocking. It would take more than $1.25 million per year to operate as a closed institution. The cost included a minimal security and custodial staff to protect the collections, insurance and severance and benefits resulting from termination of the majority of the staff. It was highly informative to discover that to operate as only a museum or a library was almost equal from an economic point of view. Of course, from an intellectual and collections viewpoint, none of these options was desirable, especially because the unique character of the Society's collections was their interrelatedness.

The Fate of the Collections

Even the mention of liquidation caused a devastating reaction in other cultural institutions. *The New York Times* reported on February 21, 1993: "Like vultures, museums and libraries across the country have begun to eye the Society's collections hungrily, ready to pick off choice pieces." We heard that institutions all around town had drawn up lists of their preferred objects. This set up an unanticipated dynamic of isolating the Society's staff from peers in the field. By the very nature of the situation, and from a pragmatic point of view, other libraries and museums needed to position themselves for the spoils of our misfortunes. In part due to an array of political pressures, virtually no other museums came forward on record in support of N-YHS, especially when we needed institutions to rally behind deaccessioning for our survival. This lack of support was perhaps best summarized by Ada Louise Huxtable in a letter to the editor (*The New York Times*, March 3, 1993), "I am ashamed of the institutions—neighborly and brotherly—that now want to 'rescue' the Society by acquiring and absorbing its assets in what looks like altruism, but is more like acquisitiveness."

Mergers

During this period, many possible mergers with other museums, libraries and cultural institutions were being explored. Frequently the staff learned about possible mergers by reading about them in the papers. The Society was reported to be investigating mergers with a variety of other institutions, including the American Museum of Natural History, New York University, the Smithsonian, the New York Public Library, the Library of Congress, the Metropolitan Museum of Art, the Museum of the City of New York and the South Street Seaport Museum. We even read that three New York State assemblymen were proposing a bill to allow the New York State Museum in Albany to take over the N-YHS.

These merger conversations, rumors and reports served to polarize the institution further. Virtually no institution was prepared to merge, take over or save both the museum and the library. When library related discussions were raised, the library felt it was to be sacrificed for the sake of the museum and vice versa. From the museum staff's point of view, the majority of earned income came from exhibitions, related programs and rights and reproductions, all produced by the museum staff. In addition, the paintings collections had been sacrificed over the years through deaccessioning in order to keep the institution alive. There was an unspoken feeling among the staff that both sides of the house should share the pain.

Disposition of individual collections was also argued for in the press. Audubon scholar Alice Ford claimed, in a *New York Times* letter to the editor, February 13, 1993, "The [Audubon] collection belongs with NYPL—original drawings, library including Auduboniana, and all archives." *New York Magazine* art critic Kay Larson said, "Keep the library intact for those who care. Keep the Audubons and Coles on the walls. And sell the rest. Or is death better?"

The staff was powerless. We could only sit back and read the news like everyone else. It is probably fair to say that from the period December 1992 through March 1993, little productive work could be accomplished in this atmosphere. Depending on different personalities, people handled the stress differently. Some staff stopped coming to work; others worked harder than ever. On February 22, the city and state collectively announced that they would make an emergency appropriation of $66,000, which would enable the Society's library to reopen for three days per week until mid-April. This would buy the advisory committee about one month to come up with a recommendation to keep the Society alive.

The Advisory Committee Report

The advisory committee report submitted on March 11, 1993 tackled many of the same issues that had been considered by the advisory committee four years earlier. However, this report focused on extreme self-help and not just a bail-out. As Cultural Commissioner Luis Cancel said in *New York Newsday*, "We're not going to help you if you can't help yourself." Although the other advisory committee report emphasized the need to sharpen the focus of the institution and to raise an endowment and balance the budget, it offered no plan to accomplish this. In fact, it was not possible without a donor base.

The resulting advisory committee plan could only be successful if all component parts were enacted. These were: 1) a new statement of mission (not only on paper but one that would be carried out in the institution's programs), 2) a $50 million endowment to be built through deaccessioning, monetization of real estate and board giving, 3) reinvigorated fund-raising and personal giving on the part of the board of trustees, and 4) a reduced operating budget requiring that institutional priorities be rigorously set and adhered to, and also requiring recurring support from both the city and the state.

Mission Statement

Central to the plan was readdressing not only the mission but how to truly focus the institution on a clear purpose. "The Historical Society needs to make better sense of itself by narrowing and redefining its mission," editorialized *The New York Times* on February 18, 1993. "What, really, should this institution be about? How can it better engage the public? And why weren't the current trustees and administrators talking about redefinition and addressing the public before the Society reached this perilous state?"

N-YHS had been incorporated as an association on February 10, 1809, for the purpose of "discovering, procuring and preserving whatever may relate to the natural, civil, literary and ecclesiastical history of the United States in general and of this state in particular."

As one of the earliest museums, it was founded as a kind of pre-Smithsonian. As other museums came into existence, the NYHS divested itself of collections that would be more appropriate elsewhere. Natural history specimens went to the American Museum of Natural History, costumes to the Metropolitan Museum of Art and Egyptian collections to the Brooklyn Museum. Clearly, the mission was overwhelmingly broad, and there had been attempts to narrow it over the years.

The staff had learned that any revision of the mission statement had a direct impact on the future of the collections and any change of mission had come to symbolize loss of collections through deaccessioning. The 1989 Advisory Committee had restated the mission: "To promote research and provide education concerning the social, political, economic and cultural history of New York City, its environs and state from the earliest times to the present, and of the American experience from the early years of the nation with primary focus on strengths of the 17th and 18th and 19th centuries." This later statement was still very broad. In particular, the phrase "the American experience" allowed for retaining virtually any object in the collection.

The most recent mission more narrowly focuses the collections on New York and defines them as "material relevant to the rich history, cultural diversity and current evolution of New York City, State and surrounding region, and those collections which have important intrinsic national significance." There was no question that the collections and purpose had to be "leaner and meaner." This time, much of the staff had a direct part in reasoning and arguing through the new mission and, in the end, agreed to all elements of it.

Deaccessioning

The staff had accepted the reality that the collections would have to be shaped and deaccessioning occur if the institution was to survive. This appeared to be the only way both to add to the endowment and to provide better care and access. The advisory committee report proposed that $20 million of the needed endowment come from sale of the collections. However, this one-time deaccessioning would occur only if $20 million was raised simultaneously through board contributions and sale of real estate. Working with the directors of the museum and library, the committee made the creative and unprecedented proposal that only those objects declined by New York public institutions would be offered elsewhere for public sale. This is something akin to the process that exists in Europe for the reclaiming of cultural property. Procedures were implemented so that utmost efforts would be made to keep all material accessible to the public in New York.

The board charged me with the task of chairing the collections committee and overseeing and ensuring that $20 million of objects were identified for deaccessioning. I believe that the staff was satisfied that every step had been taken to proceed with careful and ethical deaccessioning. Unlike the previous deaccessionings, this time the staff was thoroughly involved. Thus began the emotional process of rigorous debates about individual objects. There was a conscious effort to "share the pain" between museum and library collections so that the same reasoning would be applied to all parts of the collections and not only the paintings collections, as before. The resulting detailed proposed arrangements for disposition, agreed upon with the state attorney general, were innovative and, I believe, unique in the history of American museums.

The concept of "one-time deaccessioning" evoked widespread reaction from the public. There appeared to be at least one voice in favor of retaining each and every object. *The New York Times* ran this headline: "NEW YORK HISTORICAL SOCIETY TRIES TO LIVE BY SUBTRACTION" (March 12, 1993). The proposal to deaccession came as no shock to the outside world but was sobering nonetheless.

Real Estate

Equally controversial was the proposal to amortize the five empty house lots behind the Society in order to obtain $15 million for the endowment. The concept of selling or building on this lot had long been discussed as a valuable way of contributing to the endowment. The Society was no longer in a position to leave this asset unused. The new modest outline of a proposed building plan was received with trepidation by the local West Side community battling to control development. Upper West Side council member Ronnie Eldridge, although a supporter of efforts to save the Society, expressed her concern: "Well, if they're planning to stay in their ivory tower by building a real tower, they should expect a fight." The *Upper West Side Resident* reported, "There undoubtedly would be some people who don't want one more block of cement put into the ground."

The advisory committee report proposed that the community be involved from the very beginning to arrive at an acceptable proposal, and the board agreed. Deaccessioning was to be carried out only in consort with the real estate plan because it had long been acknowledged that $20 million to be raised as endowment through the collections would not be sufficient to achieve the operating budget. The overall plan could not succeed without the key cash component of the real estate.

Ongoing Support

Most important from the perspective of the staff, the report emphasized the need to raise ongoing operating support. The building of an endowment through collections and real estate would contribute to recurring income, but the private and public sectors would also need to make an ongoing commitment. Significantly, the board agreed to raise or contribute at least $1 million annually, and the city and state a combined $950,000. In addition, the operating budget was carefully refined and reviewed. The director of the library and I constructed a budget based on serving the collections and the public. Correctly criticized for becoming top-heavy in administration, we combined and redefined a number of positions. Public service positions and educational functions were increased and curatorial and collections positions given appropriate support. We succeeded in reducing the annual operating budget to below $5 million (at various points it had been up to almost $8 million). In addition, a bare-bones capital budget of $10 million was developed to concretely address all urgent work that had been deferred since the building was first constructed in 1904. Last, a detailed interim budget was developed for the upcoming year, which, if carefully adhered to, would allow for the above planning and for the Society to remain partially open.

Public Reaction

The advisory committee report was concrete, challenging and daring, and required staff, board and the public and private sectors to buy into it. It addressed for the first time how to achieve operating support through endowment and public funding, and proposed a specific operating budget of under $5 million, developed by the people who were to carry out the plan—the staff. "The speed with which the committee produced the plan and the political savvy with which the community and board sold it are dazzling. But every point of the plan is, at the very least, controversial," declared *New York Newsday.* An editorial in *The New York Times* said, "The advisory committee presents a plausible case for keeping a stripped down, better focused, and more manageable N-YHS. If its administrators can make the plan work, they fully deserve the kind of support from the city and state that the committee envisions." And in another opinion, the *Times* added, "Each part of the plan could be criticized and derailed by bureaucratic obstacles, but the alternative is to have nothing but a shuttered limestone monument to neglect."

The board adopted the plan. The senior staff had been involved in the speedy development of budgets: capital, operating and interim-year. The responsibility for implementation fell squarely on the shoulders of the board.

Gaining City and State Support

The next set of shock waves occurred as the institution set about gaining the required one-time support from the city and state in what was described as a fierce battle over scarce public resources. Other local cultural institutions were understandably uneasy that the N-YHS, accused of isolationism and poor management, would now receive public funds. The cultural commissioner said to *The New York Times*: "The appearance of rewarding an organization for mismanagement is something we have to be very careful about." Norma Munn, chairwoman of the New York City Arts Coalition, stated in the same article that rescuing N-YHS with $6.3 million "lacks a sense of proportion and sets a bad precedent." And a headline in the *Art Newspaper* (June 1993) said, "SUBSIDY EARNS RACIAL WRATH: HISPANIC ARTS ORGANIZATIONS OPPOSE $6.3 MILLION GRANT TO WASP INSTITUTION."

Ultimately the Historical Society won this battle. By the end of June, $12.6 million was appropriated by the city and state to help rescue the institution: $10 million for capital purposes and $2.6 million for one-time operating support. Additionally, the board of trustees contributed $110,000 to enable the library to operate through June.

Conclusion: The Future

As of June 1994, the remaining staff of 35 people is faced with formidable tasks. Some of the best staff people have left and some have stayed. A large-scale, one-time deaccessioning program must be concluded amidst a climate of criticism and concern over deaccessioning. Now that local government funding has been promised, the public's expectations have increased about programs and service, despite the fact that the overall staff is much smaller and the public programs staff has in the interim year been completely eliminated.

Three major off-site exhibitions, which raise income and visibility for the institution, also have to be produced by the same skeletal staff. Major planning for the capital program needs to be implemented. The amortization of the real estate has not begun and must be concluded quickly to add to the endowment. A dialogue must be continued between the staff and the new community advisory board. Increased contact is needed with the state attorney general. As the Society embarks on this critical year, it depends upon a staff one-quarter of its previous size to implement the demanding components of the plan. The institution still suffers from its lack of a large endowment and of an energetic board donor base. There is no unified sense of purpose.

Fundamental and urgent questions have yet to be answered. Who is the new public going to be? How will the institution distinguish itself and its audience from the Museum of the City of New York, the New York Public Library or the Metropolitan Museum of Art? How will the institution create a public and public member donor base when the highest annual attendance numbers in recent years are 92,000 (compared with several million visitors a year at the American Museum of Natural History next door)? How will collections grow through donations in an environment of deaccessioning? Even if the Society had the funding, which it does not, how will the museum and library be integrated, given the technological obstacles and the fact that museum and library operations, procedures, and users have always differed so widely?

The Author's Position

In this chapter, I have represented opinions about the Society as formulated in part through the press. I have attempted to give a sense of the barrage of issues that bombarded the staff and administration. In no way do I attempt to represent every viewpoint. My observation of staff reactions is, of course, my personal perception.

The situation at the N-YHS is so complex, and has been sustained over such a long period of time, that it can serve as a case study of an institution in virtually continual crisis. Many of the incidents touched on—deaccessioning, possible mergers with other institutions and issues about real estate, to name a few—could serve as books on their own. But I have not wished simply to suggest different approaches that might have been taken as events at the Society evolved rapidly. Rather, my intent has been to provide an accurate account of events that will serve to instruct other institutions that might face similar crises.

Last, and most important, I wish to applaud the efforts of a highly dedicated staff, the men and women who maintained their high professional standards in the face of extraordinary pressure.

A Merger in Limbo

The Collegiate Museum of Art in Wilkes-Barre, Pa.

Judith Hansen O'Toole

The idea that was to become The Collegiate Museum of Art (CMA) in Wilkes-Barre, Pa., a museum to be jointly owned and operated by King's College and Wilkes University, was first discussed in 1988. At that time, I had been director of the Sordoni Art Gallery at Wilkes University for six years; I had stayed perhaps three years beyond what I had anticipated my tenure to be when I first accepted the position. A combination of things kept me in Wilkes-Barre, including freedom to direct the gallery's course and organize exhibitions I felt were important, and a warm and appreciative audience. A department of the university, the Sordoni Art Gallery is the only professional visual arts facility in town and enjoys good community support. This was bolstered by the university administration's view of the gallery's programs as outreach, serving as goodwill for the surrounding metropolitan area.

To help guide the gallery, an advisory commission made up of prominent citizens and a few faculty members worked hard to refine and promote our mission. We had developed beyond a small university art gallery, reaching the point where we either needed to grow in physical size or turn away community interest and refocus on the campus audience. In short, we were becoming increasingly frustrated by the gallery's growth potential and the university's inability to provide for it.

The Sordoni was founded in 1972, opened its doors in 1973, and consists of a single exhibition space of about 1,200 square feet, two offices, a tiny kitchen and a storage vault. The loading dock is on the other side of the large classroom complex that houses the gallery, with several series of double doors, steps and a courtyard impeding movement from the dock to the gallery. Originally conceived as a component of the art department, the gallery soon outgrew that arrangement. I was the first full-time, professionally trained director named, and my directive was to continue courting the community, bring in high quality exhibitions, foster the growth of a modest permanent collection and do what outreach I could manage without any support staff. (When I began in 1982 I had virtually no staff other than student assistants. By 1989 I had a secretary and a part-time assistant.)

The gallery's donor, the Sordoni Foundation, had designed a state-of-the-art exhibition space with good climate-control and security systems. This enabled us to borrow significant works of art and assemble solid exhibitions, some of which later traveled to other, usually larger, institutions. The general community responded well to the blockbuster exhibitions and wanted more. Meanwhile, donors and educators wanted gallery space for displaying the permanent collection. Regional artists wanted exhibition space for their works. A small core of volunteers was weary of trying to keep up with a rapidly changing exhibition program without the guidance of an education coordinator, and of the lack of on-site space to hold meetings and classes, or even to orient a large group of visitors.

Andrew J. Sordoni III, grandson of the gallery's namesake, is a supportive benefactor who agreed that the gallery needed to grow. Sordoni was also a contributor to King's College, a rival school just six city blocks away and similar in size and curriculum to Wilkes. King's had eliminated their art department some years earlier and had begun a general program called "Experiencing the Arts" that all undergraduates were required to take. The problem was that the English faculty taught the course, which included exposure to all the arts, including the visual. This was a difficult task for a conscientious faculty, and the school began to suffer from the absence of a professional visual arts presence. The solution to these two seemingly independent problems—the need for the Sordoni to expand and the desire for King's to establish a gallery program—seemed clear. Sordoni would eventually suggest that the two schools work together on a cooperative facility that would provide more space for the Sordoni Art Gallery and bring the visual arts to the King's curriculum.

As prelude to this, on a cold, gray Saturday morning in February 1989, I toured with Mr. Sordoni a building strategically located between the two campuses and just one block from central downtown's Public Square. Built in 1912 as an Elks Club, the building could not have been more appropriate for reuse as a museum. Spacious areas with high ceilings and almost no load bearing walls had been used for balls and other entertainment. The structure was handsome in design and located within Wilkes-Barre's historic district. Daunted only by the building's size—almost 30,000 square feet (quite a jump from the Sordoni's 2,000)—I confirmed its suitability as a potential, but expensive, answer to our needs.

Quiet discussions began with key board members at Wilkes and by the end of that summer I had had many long meetings in the president's office considering the potential problems and benefits of a collaborative project. I felt it was important to warn those concerned of the high cost involved in running such a large facility—increased staff, utilities, programming costs and so on. To me, the first question to be answered was, "Is this an appropriate and responsible action for these two schools to undertake, given their modest size and the multitude of other needs expressed by their faculty and students?" With some trepidation but generally high spirits, we decided to pursue the concept.

That fall began with new responsibilities. In addition to keeping the Sordoni Art Gallery running, I needed to act as catalyst, mediator, advisor and advocate for the new museum. It was exhilarating but exhausting. I began to leave the burden of day-to-day operations to my staff. Because they did not have museum training, they were not included in much of the planning process for the new museum and this began to alienate them. My assistant left after about a year because "things were not the same as they once were." I was caught up in the excitement of the future and was insensitive to others losing control of a familiar past.

Problems also arose with my very dedicated advisory commission. They were reluctant to share the rewards of their years of hard work. The Sordoni's growing reputation and collection were a source of pride: to them, collaborating with an institution with nothing to offer in similar reputation and expertise was unwise. While they agreed that the concept was a good one, many members felt the logistics could not be worked out to the satisfaction of both principals. There was talk of charging King's College for the collective assets of the Sordoni Art Gallery in order to let them in on the program—not a good grounding for cooperation. I understood their concerns but was convinced that the benefits both schools and the surrounding community would gain from this collaboration were worth some sacrifice. This, after all, was a larger, more ambitious museum facility and program than either could hope to support independently.

Meanwhile, it was a blessing for me that the two schools had such different needs for the museum. I did not have a counterpart at King's with whom I had to consult. Wilkes's art department could talk to the King's English department without involving professional egos and territories. Had we had to merge two galleries and work with two art departments, our job would have been much more difficult.

Initially costs for the project were not seriously analyzed. The operating expenses were not so much at issue as the capital investments needed. Both King's and Wilkes were involved in capital campaigns. Both indicated they could not participate actively in another. Therefore, a small group of dedicated leaders would have to do the fund raising. The figure thrown around for renovation of the building (not based on the escalated costs of museum construction) was $3 million. It seemed an attainable figure within the economic climate of the late 1980s.

Representatives of Wilkes, King's and the Sordoni Foundation met about the project for the first time on September 1, 1989. We agreed to begin formal interinstitutional talks on establishing a collaborative museum. The Sordoni Foundation would facilitate the discussions but would not assume a long-term management role. A steering committee was organized with a representative appointed from each of the principals, including myself to represent both Wilkes and the museum.

Our prior meetings had revolved around rather abstract issues—ideas of collaboration and partnership, working toward the common good, and even defining the common good. Now we started to grapple with more mundane issues such as zoning, parking and general building maintenance. These were still exciting tasks because they made the project tangible and more within our grasp.

However, when we began discussions in earnest about the actual operation and ownership of a collaborative museum, we ran into our first problems. There were convoluted and, to me, frightening suggestions concerning the logistics of running the museum so both partners shared the costs and responsibilities. These ranged from having half the staff employed by King's and the other by Wilkes, one school to handle security and the other maintenance, one to control the galleries during certain months of the year and then the other, and other administrative nightmares! These suggestions came from otherwise rational board members who were perhaps naive to the workings of a professional museum. I realized that, as director, I could end up answering to three governing boards—those of Wilkes, King's and the new museum. We looked for other examples of collaborative ventures, hoping to find a model, and found none. The closest was the Warhol Museum being organized in Pittsburgh, but even there the Carnegie served as the umbrella organization, eliminating many, but not all, of the logistical problems. It became clear that the only functional answer was to set up a separate not-for-profit organization whose assets were owned by the trustees of the two schools, but which could operate as a single entity.

Meanwhile, we began to interview architects in the late fall of 1989 with two prominent regional firms primarily involved. Committee members decided to have an outsider review the proposals and also suggested that a consultant would be helpful in other matters. David Scott, retired director of the National Museum of American Art, had been involved in numerous building projects and is a respected museum professional. He became our advisor and agreed to come talk with us. Scott reinforced our enthusiasm for the building, its central location in town and its suitability for conversion to our proposed use. He cautioned, however, that we needed to find an architect experienced with the unique requirements of museum construction so we did not have to teach them or have them learn from our mistakes.

The firm of Dagit•Saylor in Philadelphia had recently completed the Berman Museum at Ursinus College. We had been impressed by the Berman, one of a number of institutions we visited in an effort to familiarize the nonprofessionals with the issues we would be addressing. Although Wilkes-Barre is a town where local talent must be used to ensure local support, we asked Dagit•Saylor to submit a proposal.

On March 19, 1990, the principals met again with board resolutions in hand from both King's and Wilkes endorsing their institutions' participation in the project. Both were careful to exclude financial support of the construction phase. A mission statement for the new entity was also approved and we finally had a name for the museum. After much discussion during the preceding months, we settled on The Collegiate Museum of Art in Wilkes-Barre. Obviously a compromise and, we hoped, only a working title, it said what was needed. It used the word "collegiate" to represent the academic institutions who would own it, and named the city to give it a public emphasis. It was certainly better than

"The Museum of Art of King's College and Wilkes University in Wilkes-Barre," which would have to be alternated with "The Museum of Art of Wilkes University and King's College in Wilkes-Barre" in all documents.

During the next few months we filed for status as a 501(c)3 organization. We drew up articles of incorporation along with bylaws to establish board and governance policies. In May these documents were approved, board members and officers were elected, I was appointed museum director and we were well on our way. Funds were approved to "gut" the building and Dagit•Saylor presented their design for the renovation. Approval was given to engage them as the project architects, although some members were concerned about using an "outside" firm. Later, when the project was put on hold, this choice was criticized as one of the flaws in our decision-making, even though the design proposal was excellent in both aesthetics and function.

The CMA board met quarterly, while the steering committee met more frequently. A joint faculty committee was set up to guide us in writing a detailed program document for the building, which the architects would then use as a guide. We gave civic leaders tours of the building to start generating support. We researched granting organizations and wrote a proposal to the NEH's Challenge Program. Word was spreading and interest was high.

By the time of our annual meeting in March 1991, we had a construction estimate of just over $5 million. There were various proposals for reducing costs, but all compromised either the function or the quality of the prospective museum. We decided to go ahead with no revisions. We also agreed that the board should draw up a solicitation list and begin fund raising, still feeling that we could do this ourselves. The Sordoni Foundation presented its gift of $1.5 million, which included the purchase, maintenance and gutting of the building.

Funds from the Sordoni grant paid for the building expenses. This included everything from utilities to architects' fees. The schools were providing security. Wilkes was providing my time as director, which increased to perhaps 50 percent of my time.

Fund raising was the most difficult issue. I do not enjoy asking people for money, but even I was ready to do so since the board seemed unwilling. To help with our expected solicitations, we developed a brochure describing the museum, its program and architectural plan. Again, this made the project more tangible, yet there were no specifics on the brochure—no giving levels to achieve, no "naming" opportunities. Out of several thousand printed, I believe we distributed only a few hundred.

Board members did not voice a growing sense of unease at meetings, in part because no one wanted to be the first to question the viability of the project. Politics in a tightly woven community hampered straightforward, board-level discussion of our mounting difficulties. Guests at cocktail parties and social gatherings discussed the museum with greater candor and energy than participants in board meetings. The steering committee began to feel some frustration with their inability to motivate the board. The Rev. Paul Farber, who had been both on the board and steering committee, died during a visit to South America. We did not replace him on the committee. The work of the steering committee had been completed. It was time for the board to act.

During the winter of 1992, we learned that the NEH had denied our request for a challenge grant. Endowment reviewers applauded the concept of our project. Many of their comments reflected good wishes for a project grounded in so much common sense and community goodwill. But they rightly questioned our lack of financial organization and therefore our ability to complete the project.

We continued to meet and discuss the issues, looking again at alternatives to bring the capital costs down. One suggestion was to open a temporary space, similar to the Temporary Contemporary that preceded the Museum of Contemporary Art in Los Angeles. This would begin the process of the two schools working together, and the joint faculty committee was anxious to start their collaborative program. Also, it would let the community see the value of the museum and thereby generate support. In the end, however, concerns about spending additional money and about the quality of programs at a temporary site ended those discussions.

At the fall 1992 board meeting we began to acknowledge that the fund raising could not be accomplished without the full support of both schools and their development offices. This was asking far more than either school had bargained for and was tantamount to asking two rival football squads to play as one team. After discussion, with still no one wanting to scale back, we decided to table the idea while continuing to look for donor prospects.

By this time, my staff and the faculty members involved had already essentially put the CMA on their collective back burners. The initial excitement and planning could not be sustained, and both faculty and staff were wary of expending too much energy or pinning too many hopes on what now looked like a long shot. The eyes of my assistant and secretary would glaze over during talk of the CMA; I remember wondering whether this was due to fear, indifference or lack of faith. It was also becoming clear that the CMA would do its own hiring, and since it would be owned by both schools, the full (albeit small) staff of the Sordoni might not be entirely welcomed. After a while, we no longer discussed the CMA around the office.

In December we were still struggling. Board meetings were now painful for some of us. Again, we tried to structure a capital campaign but could not get full board support. Momentum was dragging and the community was seriously questioning our ability to complete the project. So were we. But for various reasons, again, no one wanted to be the first to say it.

In January a museum I knew well and admired approached me to discuss its director-ship. Disillusioned, but still believing in the CMA, I agreed to interview. I felt like a traitor to the cause. The remaining member of the steering committee, Ben Badman, and I had become close friends through the process. We leaned on each other even when we dis-agreed about the course of events. I could not tell him or anyone else about my candidacy without compromising my commitment to the museum.

March 1993 brought our annual meeting. The timing was uncanny. I received a firm offer for the new position the weekend before the meeting. This permitted me to establish some distance from the CMA and be more frank in my comments to the board. I wanted the museum to succeed, yet I had begun to question not only its viability but my own ability as its director and leader. I had given what I could. Still, we presented a more coherent plan to begin fund raising and asked for approval. Once more, the board balked.

At that meeting we again voted to table the project, this time agreeing not to meet for one year. During that time we would monitor the building and be prepared to assess the entire project the following March.

I submitted my resignation as director of the Sordoni Art Gallery the following week. I had found that getting a taste of a larger institution through all the planning for the CMA had made it impossible to go back to administering a small university gallery, even for one year.

In retrospect, we made several, early, fundamental mistakes. We allowed ourselves to be led by an ideal vision of a collaborative museum without considering quirks of personali-ty and ego. We unrealistically banked on the determination and vision of one benefactor to carry the project through without realizing his need for collaboration and support. We were inflexible in our plans for construction and design. We continually failed to establish fund-raising goals.

With the CMA on hold, the Sordoni must now reorganize and revitalize its own pro-grams with the uncertainty of a merger in the future. The King's faculty must continue to improvise their efforts on behalf of the visual arts. We still hold out hope for The Collegiate Museum. I know what a powerful impact it would have on the region and the role model it would create for other institutions looking for similar solutions.

I grew as a director and administrator throughout the process of the CMA, learning many lessons quickly—lessons of diplomacy, vision, leadership and teamwork. In hind-sight, I am not certain we could have done things much differently given the players involved. Although the process did not conclude the way I had hoped, I gained maturity and seasoning as a director. Certainly in future projects I will place a greater emphasis on securing funding early. I might also urge scaling back on the project even though it might mean compromising my professional idealism. Finally, the experience taught me to trust my initial instincts, continue to involve as many constituents as feasible, move cautiously and pay more attention to what is written (or said) between the lines.

Remaking the Museum

The Brooklyn Children's Museum

Kathleen McLean and Suzanne LeBlanc

T his chapter has two authors: Kathleen McLean and Suzanne LeBlanc. Each of us has written from our own experience and point of view about a period of great change at The Brooklyn Children's Museum (BCM). We have emphasized our respective roles in effecting this change and our assessment of its impact on the staff and the institution. We were both hired by Mindy Duitz, the museum's director, but worked at the institution at different times and in different positions (Kathleen McLean as director of exhibitions from January 1986 through August 1988, and Suzanne LeBlanc as assistant director for program from January 1989 through August 1991).

We feel that dual authorship offers a unique perspective and a comprehensive look at two distinct phases of a pivotal period of change at an established institution. The chapter was written in collaboration, but we made no effort to write in the same style or to speak with one voice. We did, however, make a concerted effort to articulate our thoughts and experiences in a way that demonstrates a continuum in the process of change at a particular institution, and that describes each of our places on that continuum.

Part I. Intense and Rapid Change
Kathleen McLean

Don't slow down long enough to let old habits sneak back.
—Robert Waterman, *Adhocracy: The Power to Change*

When I first walked into The Brooklyn Children's Museum in the fall of 1985, I felt tired immediately. Frayed carpets and "Out of Order" signs dominated the public spaces, which were empty except for a few kids making clay pots on a folding table. The air hung heavy with the smell of chlorine from a water exhibit. And security guards repeatedly yelled at young visitors to "stop running" and "don't touch." But here and there, signs of life—a freshly painted information kiosk and a storytelling program in the cozy library—spoke of things to come. The museum was on the threshold of major change.

As director of exhibitions and publications, I was hired, along with three other new senior staff, to spearhead a change process that involved rethinking, redesigning and rebuilding the public spaces of the museum. It was a tough time for everyone involved. We were expected to make things happen fast. In a sense, we were the dynamite that shook loose an entrenched organization, implementing an incredible amount of change in a very short period of time.

This is my story of that change. It would be described very differently by others involved in the process. Considered in retrospect, the changes seem inevitable, obvious and concrete, but they never felt that way at the time. The path was never as clearly defined as it seems now, and time has leveled out the manic highs and depressing lows that we experienced individually and collectively.

There is a tendency with stories of change to start with ourselves and our own experiences, and to see ourselves as the instigators of the change. But change at The Brooklyn Children's Museum was years in the making. Founded in 1899, the museum had a rich history, a substantial collection and a tradition of innovative exhibits and programs that focused on natural and cultural history, the arts and the sciences. For many kids, the museum was an integral part of growing up in New York City.

During the 1960s, the museum moved from two Victorian residential mansions into a starkly modern building that was, in many ways, inappropriate for the museum and the neighborhood. Soon after the new museum opened, its walls of windows had to be covered with metal mesh and bars. And structural and sculptural elements in the maze-like roof garden obstructed views and created cul-de-sacs, making it a place perceived as dangerous by families in the neighborhood. Inside, columns obstructed doorways, air ducts occupied significant portions of floor space and odd nooks and crannies required intensive maintenance.

The new exhibits, called "The Learning Environment," were an interconnected construction that focused on the physical sciences, largely ignoring the museum's collection and its programming traditions. In fact, the exhibits designer seemed to view collection objects as obstructions to interactive learning. Most staff had little involvement in conceptual decisions, and therefore little investment in "The Learning Environment" program. And since the exhibits required ongoing supervision and operation, without staff interest they often languished in the galleries with "closed" signs. The education department continued to provide its own brand of programming, which in many cases had nothing to do with the exhibits, and the museum functioned more like a community center, relying on classes, workshops and programs to attract and engage people.

The museum's innovative spirit had not disappeared—it was just hidden under disjointed planning and a troublesome facility. Despite all its problems, the museum had an international reputation, a dedicated board with the capability to raise money, a solid collection of objects, an earnest staff and a core group of neighborhood kids who relied on the museum for support and guidance. In a word, the museum had "potential." It had all the ingredients for remaking a great children's museum.

Elation

My first few months on the job were invigorating and exciting. I was hired into a newly created position that allowed me a great deal of discretion and freedom to define the scope of my responsibilities. And because of the museum's mandate to change the exhibits and public spaces of the museum, I had support from the director and the senior staff. In a sense, they had completed all the preliminary planning they could, and were waiting for an exhibits plan to bring everything together.

The new development director had put in place a strong fund-raising strategy and was ready to capitalize on innovative projects. The new education director was reshaping her department to support museum-wide programming themes, and was ready to assign staff to participate in exhibit development. The new director of public relations and government affairs was organizing a strong base of community support. The curator of collections was excited about being able to focus exhibitions around the museum's collections once again. Staff in all areas of the museum expressed enthusiasm and a commitment to change. We were surrounded by opportunities.

Depression

The months that followed were slow and difficult, filled with seemingly endless limitations. Not only did we have to overhaul the entire facility—how it looked and functioned—but we also had to change the way staff thought about the organization and their role within it. Although many people voiced a need for change and envisioned a dynamic future for the organization, they were not so excited when it came to changing their own behaviors and assumptions. More than once, I heard that the problem was in someone else's department or was someone else's responsibility.

For me, this resistance to change was embodied in the public spaces. Despite repeated meetings and memos requesting changes, heavy folding tables used for public programs continued to be stacked up against the exhibits; the live animal displays were in a perpetual state of disrepair (it was not uncommon to see dead fish and animals in the display tanks); and dark stains from repeated applications of insecticide continued to appear throughout the galleries, although this didn't seem to deter the ever-present cockroaches.

Behind the scenes, tools and equipment continued to disappear. Discarded materials, including drums of toxic fumigants, piled up in the stairwells and throughout the workshops. Dirt from the galleries above continuously sifted through cracks in the floors onto staff desks and equipment.

The new senior management team knew that the organization needed to improve all of its operations and services. Yet we underestimated the effort it would take to change peoples' behaviors and values while at the same time creating opportunities for new ones.

Taking Action

Before we could develop a solid plan for the future, we needed to look at the past and present. We revisited the original museum mission and all subsequent ones in order to familiarize ourselves with the history of the place. We analyzed the assumptions of the organization and tried to clarify the underlying problems the museum was facing. We spent a lot of time talking, questioning, and talking some more. I met with almost every staff person in the exhibitions, education, collections and maintenance/security departments, to better understand their visions for a new exhibition program.

My first step was to expand the exhibitions and publications department, which meant redirecting resources from other departments. All senior staff agreed that over the next few years, exhibitions should be given top priority. As positions in other departments were vacated, they were reallocated. Some positions were simply shifted to exhibitions. Within a year, the department had more than tripled its size.

At the same time, we needed to take immediate concrete actions that would energize people, create small successes, and start the change process in motion. We set up a "We Are Changing" exhibit in the museum's entry, describing our plans to change the galleries and exhibits and soliciting suggestions from visitors and staff alike. We needed to sell the process, both internally and externally, and we capitalized on the little changes, showing that we were indeed changing.

We began by developing small exhibitions on short time frames with tiny budgets. Some were conceived, designed and built in five weeks or less. Many of these first exhibitions were chosen simply because of visitor and staff interest or collection strength. They were all produced internally and were experiments in team building as well as exhibit development and design. At the same time, we replaced one large semi-permanent exhibition with a new one, using a consulting designer and exhibit builder. These professionals provided a model for design and fabrication that exhibit staff later critiqued, identifying what they thought was successful and not so successful in the process. This helped to create a framework for an appropriate exhibit development process for the museum.

Within the first six months, we had developed a new museum mission and a conceptual framework for programs that focused on exhibitions and created a strategy for making future programming decisions. We developed guidelines for the maintenance of all public spaces, conducted training on visitor-staff interaction, created systems for maintaining inventories and monitoring equipment and supplies, and developed schedules for security and maintenance.

Yearning for the Past

With the realization that these changes would affect every person and activity in the organization, staff began to talk more and more fondly about "the old days." Many people had worked at the museum for 10 years or more, and they shared group experiences and behaviors that had been accepted over time. "We've always done it that way" and "It used to be better" were recurring themes.

Some staff who had expressed excitement at the prospect of change were resistant when confronted with a sense of loss. Response to the new plans ranged from disinterest to hostility. Many of the "old guard" were antagonized by the aggressive personalities and persistent visions of the new staff. The new people—outspoken and on a mission—were given most of the resources, attention and credibility. Not surprisingly, people who had been with the museum a long time felt demoralized, ignored and discredited in the rush for change. Many became defensive. Even those who supported the change process had no idea how traumatic it would be.

Gradual Buy-In

Despite these deeply traumatic feelings, the growing exhibition program provided successful new experiences for people. And each new person hired brought vital energy and enthusiasm, creating an environment in which more and more staff "bought in" to the change process. The buy-in was evident in little things. People began to volunteer for exhibit team assignments. They stayed at work beyond their eight hours—unusual in a place that was ordinarily empty by 5:05 p.m. (During installation of our first big exhibition, people stayed all night to get the work done.)

Previously, few people in the organization saw themselves as part of a larger profession with its own body of knowledge and standards. Because staff were isolated from the field, we focused a great deal of initial energy on training. "Doing It Right," for example, was a three-year project that trained staff in label writing and evaluation and culminated in the production of a label workbook. In the exhibition "Dr. Dimension and the Rulers of the Universe," we experimented with all kinds of labels, typefaces, materials and methods of presentation. We learned by our mistakes and improved the exhibition as we went along. In other exhibitions, we experimented with display techniques, combining objects and interactives, and developing multidisciplinary themes.

Education staff training focused on visiting museums throughout the New York City area, observing their programs and discussing educational methods with colleagues. Programs gradually began to tie in more closely with exhibit themes and school curricula. In conjunction with "Dr. Dimension," for example, education staff presented a series of curriculum-based programs that interpreted elements of the exhibition and expanded upon the concept of measurement.

Relentless Moving Forward

For those people who thrive in an open-ended, experimental atmosphere, the changes were invigorating and exciting, no matter how difficult. A number of staff jumped right in and seemed to blossom overnight when assigned to the new projects and activities. But for those people who prefer an environment with more structure and clearly defined goals, life at the museum was chaotic and hellish. Things changed so quickly that many staff couldn't get a sense of where they might fit in.

This wasn't helped by our long-range planning process. From the beginning, the senior management team worked together without rigidly defined roles. We were all passionate about the possibilities for the museum—we lived and breathed it. We were envisioning a future. But often, our vision was not communicated to the rest of the staff. Our long-range planning got off to a good start when we hired an experienced consultant to lead a weekend retreat with senior staff and the board of trustees. But the consultant was not retained long enough to help us develop a strategic plan. Each department head created a separate plan, each of which was sketchy at best. Many staff did not get a chance to participate in the process, and we never integrated the individual department plans into one institutional plan. This left the program departments locked in an adversarial relationship, each competing for power and limited resources.

Despite these problems, within three years we had formed an exhibitions department; replaced all of the permanent exhibits; developed 12 new exhibitions conceived, designed, and built by a combination of existing and new staff; revised the museum mission and created a conceptual framework that gave a cohesive focus to all museum programs; upgraded all the systems and procedures in the museum; and designed a dense five-year plan for exhibitions.

Looking Back

By the time I left The Brooklyn Children's Museum two and a half years later, a major transformation had already occurred, and the change process had a momentum of its own. Innovative exhibitions and programs had restored the museum's credibility in the eyes of the public and donors. Attendance was up. Accreditation was imminent. But change came at a price. Within a three-year period, four of the new senior staff had left the museum, exhausted. And nearly half of the rest of the staff of 80 had departed, replaced by new hires. In talking to colleagues who shared this experience with me, we were surprised to discover how painful our memories still were, how difficult it was to reconstruct this particular past. But we were also surprised by how quickly we could rekindle our enthusiasm and passion for our vision of The Brooklyn Children's Museum.

It is easy to wonder, in retrospect, if a more gradual, more gentle and evolutionary process could have created the necessary momentum for change. I doubt it. For this particular organization, intense and rapid change was probably a good thing, no matter how traumatic. But after a period of upheaval, there must come a time of stabilization, reevaluation and reorganization—a period of bridge-building and integration. For those of us who were not part of that next phase, we can take pride in knowing that we envisioned a new Brooklyn Children's Museum and created an innovative exhibition plan that is now, nine years later, almost complete.

Having undergone this difficult process of change, I have developed some guidelines for institutions facing similar situations:

- change must be founded on vision
- there must be a commitment and passion for the vision
- avoid haste and ruthlessness, but also hesitation and conservatism
- create clear guidelines accessible to everyone
- ensure clear communication
- create small, concrete actions that can provide successes
- be willing to take risks, to challenge yourself and others
- expect to fail along the way; welcome the failures and learn from them
- understand the nature of the environment
- look beyond the immediate
- know that you can't do it alone
- evaluate and revise the process

(I would like to thank Kathleen Fluegel and Wendy Abel-Weiss for their thoughtful comments and advice in preparing this chapter.)

Part II. Integrating Change
Suzanne LeBlanc

When I arrived at The Brooklyn Children's Museum for my interview with the director in September of 1988, a tour of the exhibits revealed an institution clearly in the middle of a great deal of experimentation and change. I saw, on the one hand, sophisticated exhibitions combining artifacts and interactives in new and interesting ways, and everywhere evidence of new things being tried out. On the other hand, I saw old unlit displays, unfinished and broken exhibits, and large empty spaces where exhibits should have been. This tour was prophetic. The museum was in the middle of enormous change—poised to accomplish great things, but stuck and somewhat shell-shocked by the pace and process.

I was hired by Mindy Duitz in January of 1989 to fill a newly created position, an assistant director of the museum with broad responsibility for all programmatic areas of the institution: exhibitions, education and collections. I knew when I accepted the position that three department heads, including the directors of the exhibition and education departments, had left within the previous six months. It was obvious to me soon after I arrived that staff morale was low, and that unresolved power struggles in the departments I was now responsible for were paralyzing forward movement.

Because my position was new, I was, with the director, crafting my role from scratch. To do this effectively, I needed a clear picture of the museum's history, mission, current organizational structure and staff dynamics. It was important to understand the museum's place in the community, its unique character, its problems and successes. Clearly, and most immediately, it was critical to understand the process of change to date, and individual staff members' perception of that process.

Assessment

I resolved to give myself a month to read, observe, interview, assess and evaluate before making any significant changes or decisions. I read official, finished documents such as proposals, the museum's long-range plan, departmental goals and objectives, as well as more informal and internal documents such as recommendations written by some of the department heads who had recently left, meeting notes and staff complaint letters and memos. I wanted to steep myself in the language of how The Brooklyn Children's Museum presented itself to the world, especially given the influence of my 15-year employment at The Children's Museum in Boston. I knew I would not be helpful or effective if I automatically responded to situations with "At the Children's Museum in Boston we. . . ."

I individually interviewed all permanent full- and part-time staff in the three program departments, offering them the opportunity to discuss their own jobs and professional goals. I opened up the dialogue to include how well or poorly they saw their own departments functioning and why. I also asked for input into what someone in my position could accomplish and contribute.

Although these interviews were time-consuming, they proved to be invaluable. I credit this process with getting me off to the right start in what was not the easiest job situation to be walking into. The interviews accomplished three overarching goals: they provided me with the information I needed to craft a clear, strong framework for my position and decision-making; they provided a much-needed outlet for staff to voice, in an appropriate forum, their anger, fears, insecurities, opinions and dissatisfactions, as well as their hopes for the museum's future; and they provided the foundation for working relationships between myself and staff.

During this assessment period I also attended meetings with the express purpose of observing staff dynamics, especially at meetings that involved more than one department. Particularly instructive was one meeting—called after a major exhibition had opened—to discuss problems with the exhibition development process. This meeting, held the day after I arrived at the museum, was attended by representatives from the three program departments, and was not led or mediated by anyone. It quickly deteriorated into non-productive accusations, further reinforcing the interdepartmental staff problems the meeting was theoretically called to address. This meeting quickly made evident the need for my position in the institution as well as some of the major structural and morale problems in my departments that needed to be addressed.

Following my month-long assessment period I saw three major directions for my work: improving staff morale, creating a program division with a unified vision, and refining, clarifying and institutionalizing the new systems and processes that *had* been experimented with. A number of exhibit, publication and education projects were in various stages of completion, and proved to be fertile training ground for this work.

Staff Morale

It became quickly evident that the change process initiated by the director and given shape and accelerated by Kathy McLean and other department heads who had since left, could not move forward without an improvement in staff morale. It was time for the healing phase of the change process.

When the directors of the exhibitions and education departments left the museum, they were replaced by acting department directors who moved up within the institution and eventually became the new department heads. Individually and collectively with the curator of collections, they would prove to be critical players in improving the way staff viewed the institution and their place within it. I worked intensively with each of the new department heads to develop and support their sense of themselves as leaders, and with all three to create a strong team of people who would be trusted by staff to be both advocates for their individual departments as well as leaders who would take the welfare of the entire institution into consideration when making decisions.

A key component of my role as an assistant director of the museum for the program division was that I was invested with the authority to make decisions and mediate conflicts about program department roles, power issues and priorities, but at the same time was not a member of any of the three departments. This sense that I was making decisions based on an understanding of the needs of the three program departments and with the good of the entire institution in mind was of paramount importance in allowing the divisions and rifts among departments to mend.

Although The Brooklyn Children's Museum had a rich history and was going through an exciting stage in its institutional development, a number of staff felt professionally isolated by the museum's location in Brooklyn, and stuck in a building that in many ways was hard to work in. For instance, two levels of offices were built underground and had no windows. The museum's location and resulting identity as a community institution, however, was what made it unique. Part of the healing process involved "leading with" and developing a sense of pride about what was different, special and unique about this museum's location.

Turning a perceived negative on its head, staff developed increased programming for unaccompanied neighborhood children and teens, and developed family forums for parents in the neighborhood. The museum acquired funding for these programs, staff spoke at conferences about them, and the developing sense of institutional pride helped unify and heal what had been a badly divided staff.

Creating A Program Division

The pace of rapid change and experimentation in exhibition development and design described by Kathy McLean succeeded in transforming the role of exhibits in the museum's presentation of content to the public, as well as the role of the exhibit department within the institution. This transformation was exciting, but also unsettling to many. Conflicts over priorities, power and decision-making were rampant within and among the program departments.

The challenge we were presented with was to create one entity with a unified vision out of three competing departments. The symbolism of my title and role (assistant director for program) helped enormously to give voice to and reinforce this goal. Staff were exhausted, tired of the conflict and eager for new direction. The director gave me support when needed, but also the autonomy and authority I needed to be effective.

The three program department heads and I met weekly to plan, discuss and sometimes argue our way through to a structure and direction for a new program division with three distinct but interrelated departments unified by a shared vision. If we could not agree on certain issues, I made the final decision. We agreed that disagreements among us would not be brought back to staff. We created a team that staff, for the most part, trusted and relied on to provide leadership and solve problems.

A monthly program division meeting was instituted, with about 25 people attending each month. This meeting was a forum to share information, conduct staff training, teach each other more about what each of us did and build excitement about the museum's accomplishments and plans for the future. For example, a graphic designer used the meeting to describe (with slides and in a humorous way) the process copy had to go through to get turned into a brochure. We had been having problems getting copy turned in on time to meet deadlines. This monthly meeting was very successful in improving communication among departments and in creating a sense of shared goals. Sometimes staff in the finance, administrative and maintenance and security departments would attend—a testament to the meeting's success at building cohesion.

Implementation

The next step in the change process was to evaluate, refine, clarify and institutionalize the new systems and processes, in particular the exhibition development process. Two major exhibit projects ("Animals Eat" and "Night Journeys") and several smaller ones were in varying stages of development when I arrived at the museum, as well as a major curriculum project and a substantial publication (*Doing It Right*). We used these projects to carefully craft and model a new way of working together.

Using as a model the written guidelines for the exhibition development process produced by Kathy McLean and her team, we first spent quite a bit of time clarifying roles and identifying staff who would best fill these roles. Earlier, in the excitement of opening up the exhibit development process to as many people as possible, roles were more fluid and expectations for involvement sometimes could not be met.

We identified a weak link in the process and strengthened a role we called the concept developer. This role soon became a full-time position requiring specific skills. In addition to hiring a full-time concept developer, we identified two other staff with the skills and interest to fill this role, and carved out real time in their jobs to enable them to be effective.

The role of the weekly exhibit team meeting was refined as we went along. Previously, many of the exhibit ideas were collaboratively developed at this meeting, causing endless arguments and delays, and sometimes lack of focus. Now, with the concept developer doing prior research and bringing developed ideas to be discussed, challenged and refined, meetings became more productive and streamlined. Discussion of ideas was still loud and lively, but took place within a framework that provided structure and focus.

The review process was clearly communicated and occurred early and often. This eliminated the possibility of project staff working for months in a direction that ultimately would be unacceptable to the museum. The three program department heads were involved in the review process, as well as the museum director and I. The review process was structured, but like everything else during this period, we evaluated and refined the structure as we went along.

My role in the process was four-fold: to work with and oversee the work of the concept developer; to mediate and make decisions when agreement could not be reached in the exhibit team; to be observant of the process and to problem-solve and make changes when things were not going well; and to provide quality control of the product throughout.

Looking Back

As I look back on this time period now, several things seem important to emphasize. First, I could not have done what I did without the support of the director. She created my position and invested it with real authority. In choosing Kathy and me at different times in the stages of remaking the museum, and in giving us different roles, I believe she chose wisely and well. My position often seemed to me to be a perfect match of institution, time and place. I love puzzles and problem-solving; I am comfortable with making decisions; and I am trained in psychology, mediation and conflict resolution. These are all things that were required of my position at the time I joined The Brooklyn Children's Museum.

Second, my accomplishments and those of my staff followed naturally from those of Kathy and her staff. The remaking of The Brooklyn Children's Museum took place on a continuum. For each of us it was necessary to understand what had come before. I believe that each of us was successful, in part, to the degree to which we learned from and built on what had preceded us. I argue strongly for taking time to understand institutional history.

Third, the actions I took and the decisions I made spring from my philosophy of management. This includes a belief in the importance of process, of decisiveness, of clarity of communication and organizational structure, as well as a belief in the need to be flexible enough to constantly assess, refine and recreate. It was this emphasis on creating, evaluating and modifying our process that kept the environment of the museum dynamic while we went about the difficult work of producing exhibits, curriculum projects and publications.

Finally, The Brooklyn Children's Museum produced several high quality and award-winning exhibitions and publications during the period of its remaking described by Kathy and me. These include "Night Journeys: An Exhibition About Sleep and Dreams," which won the AAM Curators Award; "Animals Eat: Different Feasts for Different Beasts," which was funded by the National Science Foundation (NSF) and is being toured by the Association of Science-Technology Centers (ASTC); and "Doing It Right: A Publication About Improving Exhibit Labels," which is sold by AAM and ASTC's publication services. This work, and the groundbreaking work the museum continues to do, is a testament to the efforts to revitalize and redirect the institution, as well as to the resilience and determination of all the staff who participated in the process.

Part III. Some Lessons

The process of writing this chapter required us to be in turn reflective, impassioned, analytical and self-critical. We examined our leadership and management styles as well as the internal and external forces that acted upon our particular situations at the museum. What did we learn?

We find it instructive to note the commonalities of our views and experience, as well as the differences. We both describe being hired for newly created positions in which we were given wide discretion and freedom by the director to define the scope of our responsibilities. Each of us clearly felt comfortable with this, acted upon it and consider it an important factor in our effectiveness at impacting the environment at The Brooklyn Children's Museum. That we were hired to fill newly created positions also meant that we were more often free from rigid expectations on the part of staff about how we should behave in those positions.

Vision, and passion for that vision, comes up in each of our stories. It was one of the key forces that propelled the change forward. Commitment to a vision keeps the focus of thought and activity on the process to be undertaken to achieve that vision. It helps keep the difficulties and failures in perspective, and enables them to be used as a learning tool.

Both of us make a case for learning and understanding institutional history. This helps put action and behavior in context. It allows one to more easily depersonalize conflicts, and to more effectively utilize them to accomplish desired goals. Conflicts openly and productively dealt with can rapidly move an institution forward, but only with the necessary training and expertise in conflict management.

Each of us describes spending quite a bit of time talking and meeting with staff. We both feel strongly this was essential to the quality of our institutional assessments and to the development of effective plans of action.

An openness to experimentation, evaluation and revision and an emphasis on process guided both of us in our work. We modeled this openness and emphasis on process as we went about the business of bringing about and integrating change, and producing quality exhibitions and programs. We feel this is essential to creating and maintaining a dynamic institution.

The differences in our approach, styles and emphases are every bit as important and instructive as those we share. One of us (Kathleen) talks more about experimentation, institutional transformation, rapid and intense change. The other (Suzanne) talks more about organizational structure, integrating change, the healing of staff morale. Would we have been able to act differently if our situations were reversed? If Suzanne had been hired first and faced the situation Kathy was faced with, how would the dynamics have changed? Would she have been able to be as effective? What if Kathy had been hired as assistant director for program rather than director of exhibitions? What role did our titles and the existing organizational structure play in how we were perceived and in how staff responded to us?

While we are not sure of the answers to these questions, we both feel certain that the way in which each of us approached the institutional environment we were faced with, and the roles each of us played, effectively addressed the problems and potential of the situation, time and place we found ourselves in. What is clear is that a thoughtful and comprehensive institutional needs assessment must precede and guide decisions about embarking on a change process as dramatic as was undertaken at The Brooklyn Children's Museum.

Bibliography

Management literature is always changing. The original bibliography, researched during 1985, has been augmented by current material that can be found in good public libraries. Interestingly, a recent search has not revealed a book written on the same subject, so only portions of the books listed below are useful or relevant to the topics in this volume.

If upon reading this book the reader wishes to see what is most current, the library categories that have proven most fruitful are those listed under organizational behavior and organizational change. When browsing through the shelves, the call numbers 658.406 and 302.35 have yielded the most interesting volumes. The *Harvard Business Review* usually can be found in the main libraries of cities and towns.

This bibliography is limited to only one listing per author. However, other books written by the same author may prove to be helpful to your special interest or need. A search by author is recommended.

Some publishers specialize in management issues. In particular, books published by Jossey-Bass in their management series are straightforward in style, easy to understand and often have helpful specific suggestions.

Elaine Heumann Gurian

Suggested Reading List

Beckhard, Richard, and Harris, Reuben T. *Organizational Transitions: Managing Complex Change.* Reading, Mass: Addison-Wesley, 1987.

Belasco, James A. *Teaching the Elephant to Dance: The Manager's Guide to Empowering Change.* New York: Crown, 1990.

Conner, Daryl. *Managing at the Speed of Change: How Resilient Managers Succeed and Prosper Where Others Fail.* New York: Villard Books, 1993.

Cooper, Cary L., and Marshall, Judi, eds. *White Collar and Professional Stress.* Chichester, N.Y.: John Wiley & Sons, 1980.

DeVille, J. *The Psychology of Leadership.* New York: Mentor, 1984.

Drucker, Peter. *Managing in Turbulent Times.* New York: Harper & Row, 1980.

Duncan, K. D., Gruneberg, M. M., and Wallis, D., eds. *Changes in Working Life, Proceedings of an International Conference on Changes in the Nature and Quality of Working Life.* Chichester, N.Y.: John Wiley & Sons, 1980.

Hackman, J. Richard, Lawler, Edward E. III, and Porter, Lyman W., eds. *Perspectives on Behavior in Organizations.* New York: McGraw-Hill, 1983.

Harshman, Carl L., and Phillips, Steven L. *Teaming Up: Achieving Organizational Transformation.* Amsterdam: Pfeifer & Co., 1994.

House, J. S. *Work Stress and Social Support.* Reading, Mass.: Addison-Wesley, 1981.

Kanter, Rosabeth Moss, Stein, Barry A., and Jick, Todd D. *The Challenge of Organizational Change: How Companies Experience It and Leaders Guide It.* New York: The Free Press, 1992.

Kets de Vries, Manfred F. R., and Miller, Danny. *Unstable at the Top: Inside the Troubled Organization.* New York: New American Library, 1987.

Lawrence, Paul R. "How to Deal with Resistance to Change." *Harvard Business Review* 47 (January-February 1969): 4.

Leavitt, Harold J., Pondy, Louis R., and Boje, David, eds. *Readings in Managerial Psychology,* 3d ed. Chicago: University of Chicago Press, 1980.

Levinson, Harry. *Organizational Diagnosis.* Cambridge, Mass.: Harvard University Press, 1972.

Lippitt, Gordon L., Langseth, Peter, and Mossop, Jack. *Implementing Organizational Change.* San Francisco: Jossey-Bass, 1985.

Lorsch, Jay W., ed. *Handbook of Organizational Behavior.* Englewood Cliffs, N.J.: Prentice-Hall, 1987.

Marshall, Judi, and Cooper, Cary L., eds. *Coping with Stress at Work, Case Studies from Industry.* London: Gower, Hants, 1981.

Mohrman, Allan M., Jr., Mohrman, Susan Albers, Ledford, Gerald E., Jr., Cummings, Thomas G., Lawler, Edward E. III, et al. *Large-Scale Organizational Change.* San Francisco: Jossey-Bass, 1989.

Nadler, D. A., Gerstein, M. S., and Shaw, R. B., eds. *Organizational Architecture: Designs for Changing Organizations.* San Francisco: Jossey-Bass, 1992.

Smith, Peter B. *Group Processes and Personal Change.* London: Harper & Row, 1980.

Zander, Alvin. *Making Groups Effective.* San Francisco: Jossey-Bass, 1983.

Index